INTERNET QUEST

101 Adventures Around the World Wide Web

by Catherine Halloran Cook
and Janet McGivney Pfeifer

Incentive Publications, Inc.
Nashville, Tennessee

For Phil
and
for Michael

Illustrated by Gayle S. Harvey
Cover by Marta Drayton and Gayle S. Harvey
Edited by Angela Reiner and Jennifer J. Streams

Library of Congress Catalog Card Number: 99-075427
ISBN 0-86530-456-4

PRINTED IN THE UNITED STATES OF AMERICA
www.incentivepublications.com

Guide to the Quest

INTRODUCTION

There is no greater single source of information than the Internet. Where we once diligently searched for facts in a set of encyclopedias, we now must learn to maneuver our way through the World Wide Web. Instead of scouring outdated dusty pages for information, we can go online to view interesting exhibits and learn up-to-the minute facts from experts. We can learn how to make a television documentary from filmmakers at PBS or about the latest developments in modern flight from the Smithsonian's Air and Space Museum. However, it can be difficult and time consuming to navigate without a map. The purpose of *Internet Quest* is to provide that map and introduce children to the wealth of knowledge on the Internet by sending them on a guided quest through the World Wide Web.

Internet Quest contains 101 websites that cover topics of interest to elementary school children in grades 3-6. Each entry contains a website description, address, and three questions about the content of the site. Children need to explore the site to find the answers to the questions. Searching for the answers to the Quest questions will help students develop valuable Internet research skills. This approach can teach children to regard the Internet as a powerful research tool. In an effort to ensure readers will be able to access current websites on the Internet, the authors have created a website readers can visit should they discover a web address referenced in this book is no longer valid. The address of this website is http://members.aol.com/iaforkids/InternetAdventures/index.htm. This site also contains the links to the sites mentioned in this book!

Begin your *Internet Quest* by visiting **Safety on the Web** at http://www.safekids.com. The Safe Kids Website educates parents and children about the possible problems lurking in cyberspace by presenting the risks of randomly surfing the net and providing specific guidelines for parents on how to reduce these risks. Read *My Rules for Cyber Space* and print out the six basic rules of Internet safety. The site also offers a Directory of Parental Control, links to articles on Internet safety, and links to safe search engines for children. Another good site to visit to gain information on web safety is www.getnetwise.com. Some people advocate the use of filters, or screens, that eliminate access to mature and inappropriate sites. Others believe that filters block free speech and that children need to learn how to use the Internet in a responsible and appropriate manner. Whatever your view as an adult, be sure your children know how to safely navigate the web.

Chat rooms, while a great place to exchange ideas, are not places to give out personal information. Be sure to develop and discuss chat room rules of safety with your children. Write down your own rules and post them near the computer where they can be seen at all times. Practice the safety guidelines by presenting your children with hypothetical situations, and explore solutions together so that your kids will know what to do if they find themselves in a questionable situation. These are important issues that need to be addressed at home and in the classroom before embarking on *Internet Quest*.

As you journey through the Internet, be sure to experiment with research tools along the way. One way is to use search engines (see *Tips and Terms*). Another way is to follow links from a website that you have used and liked. For example, if you are researching bugs, you might start out by using MetaCrawler and typing in "Bugs." After you have found a "bug" site that you like, follow the links from within that site to other sites. It's a great way to discover a variety of interesting websites.

Good luck on your *Internet Quest*!

INTERNET TIPS AND TERMS

The World Wide Web, Internet, or **Cyberspace** refers to the electronic connection or link of computers around the world via cables and modems.

Modem is the device that transmits information for computers to and from the Internet. The higher the modem speed, the faster the transmission time. The modem connects to the World Wide Web (WWW) through a Web Browser and an Internet Service Provider (ISP).

Web Browser is the program your computer uses to retrieve, read, and process the information available on other websites. Your browser (the most widely used being Microsoft Explorer and Netscape Navigator) provides you with e-mail and other tools for making the Internet easier to use. The browser has the following features which make the Internet user-friendly:

> **Bookmark** stores a website's address in a folder for easy access.
>
> **Maximize** is used to enlarge a website's screen to make it easier to read.
>
> **Minimize** is used to reduce a website's screen in order to look at other programs or pages without leaving a website.
>
> **Back** is used to back through links and pages that you have previously viewed during current Internet sessions.
>
> **Forward** is used to flip forward through links and pages previously viewed during current Internet sessions.

Internet Service Provider (ISP) is the company you use to provide you with access to the Internet. America Online (AOL) and CompuServe are some of the more widely used ISPs. The service may be a portal (providing channel routes to other sources on the web) or a service provider that provides only a connection to the Internet and leaves it to you to find your own information on the web.

Website and **web page** are the places on the Internet that you "visit." People, businesses, and government agencies create and post a web page, or a website made up of many pages, on the Internet. Typing in web addresses accesses the websites.

Web address is the address you type into your web browser to go to a specific page on the Internet. Most addresses are case sensitive—the address must be typed exactly as it appears in either upper case or lower case letters. Some websites do not allow for error when it comes to locating an address.

Links are websites easily accessed by clicking a keyword, title or phrase within another address. For example, a website about ants provides access or links to other sites related to the topic "ants." Instead of typing in the new website address, you can click on the pre-addressed title and let the browser take you there. A search engine can be used to find links to topics of interest on the web.

Search engines are programs on the Internet designed to locate websites that pertain to keywords or listed topics. For example, Metacrawler is the search engine we used most often when researching this book. We typed in a key word or topic at the Metacrawler website and the Metacrawler search engine "crawled" around the World Wide Web (in a matter of seconds) and located websites related to the topic. It then provided links and described those links in order of relevance to the topic. We followed the links to find appropriate websites. This site is efficient and comprehensive, but it is not a child-safe search engine.

Child-safe search engines are search engines designed to provide links to child-safe sites and weed out inappropriate websites. Adults need to be aware that website designers can manipulate names in their web pages so that search engines will retrieve their website. For example, http://www.whitehouse.gov takes you to the White House in the United States. However, http://www.whitehouse.com is a pornographic site. Child-safe search engines will help prevent these unwanted links from appearing in your search results, but they will not always be 100% effective. Also, remember that when you choose these child-safe search engines or filters, you will be denied access to many sites which may be suitable for children.

Delete Temporary Internet Files is a function used to delete files you are not using in order to speed up transmission time. Your computer will temporarily store the information gathered when on the Internet. Periodically delete your temporary Internet files to keep the computer from storing a huge surplus of information.

We are affected by computers every day! Did you know that the supermarket scanner and ATM machine are both computers? Do you know where computers began? They began nearly 5,000 years ago with the abacus. The abacus was followed by the calculator, which led to the development of the first modern computer, introduced during World War II. Pioneers in the microcomputer industry were Apple Computer, Commodore, IBM, and Radio Shack. Computers are now faster, smarter, and smaller than ever before. Fifth generation computers are now being developed and tested. These computers may be able to accept spoken instructions and translate foreign languages. What do you wish *your* computer could do?

All About Computers

Link With Kids Around the World

Website:

Kid Link

Address:

http://www.kidlink.org

Kidlink, an organization dedicated to opening up a global conversation for kids, is available in 16 languages. To join, kids must answer four questions about what they want to be when they grow up and how they can make the world a better place. The **Kidscafe** provides e-mail addresses and keyboxes needed to communicate with other kids in the language areas. Find out what projects kids within a language area are participating in at **Kidproj. Kidforum** lists topics and times for safe online discussions supervised by an adult moderator. This is a fantastic way for kids to broaden their views on life and get to know kids from around the world. There is even an art exchange where kids can post their work in the art gallery. Since its inception, over 175,000 kids from over 131 countries have participated.

Quest questions:

1. When was **Kidlink** founded?

   _____

2. In what country is the *Kidlink Society* based?

   _____

3. Name the six world areas that **Kidlink** has represented.

   _____

Surf Monkey™:
An Internet Guide

Website:

Welcome to Surf Monkey™—
Browser and Internet Guide for Kids

Address:

http://www.surfmonkey.com

Welcome to SurfMonkey, billed as "the first Web Browser designed just for kids." The site has links to over one million child-safe sites, so there is something for everyone! The browser tries to filter out inappropriate and mature sites, so there is a good chance that you are going to a safe site. (Always remember the safety rules and be careful!) The web designers have made it easy to find what you are looking for. There is a spot to search for a topic, both in their own **Starsites Directory**, and throughout the Web. If you don't know exactly what you are looking for, there is a nice list of categories to choose from. **Playful** (fun stuff, sports) **Newsworthy** (news, weather), **Artsy** (arts, books), **Starstruck** (TV and movies), and **Spacey** (planets, the universe) are just a few. **The Top 20 Destinations** are in a separate category; be sure to recommend a website if you think it belongs in the **SurfMonkey** database!

Quest questions:

1. What sort of information is listed under the **Playful** page of the site?

   _____

2. How do you recommend a site be included in the **Spacey** directory?

   _____

3. What art museum listed in the **Artsy** directory is described as one of the most famous and biggest art museums in the world?

   _____

What Does That Mean?

Website:

What Is . . .

Address:

http://www.whatis.com

Becoming familiar with all the terms used for computers, the Internet, and the technology that goes with them can be confusing. Find the answers to your technology questions at **Whatis.com**. Start with the basics like **What is the Internet** and move on to more complicated and detailed terms as you progress in the technology world. Go to **25 Ways to Use Whatis** as a starting point for the site and once you have become familiar with the lay-out, begin your search. **The Top Twenty** lists the most frequently asked questions from the previous week, along with links to the answers. There are recommended books as well as a page devoted to other technology websites. This is a great resource for your exploration of the Internet.

Quest questions:

1. What is TCP/IP?

   _____

2. What are Steps 1 and 2 in creating a website?

   _____

3. Where was the world's smallest abacus developed?

   _____

14

One of the most exciting things about using the Internet is the multi-media capabilities that continue to improve. Many of the websites you visit will tell you if you need a "plug-in." Plug-ins, such as QuickTime from Apple, Macromedia's Shockwave, and Network's Real Audio will help your computer come alive with music, animation, and video. Each website you visit will tell you if you need a particular plug-in, and in most cases will allow you to download the plug-in from their site. These downloads are usually free! Downloading can take time, but it is well worth the wait!

Art and Music

15

Art
Adventures

Website:

A. Pintura: Art Detective

Address:

http://www.eduweb.com/pintura/

Go on an art adventure with A. Pintura as he tries to discover the creator of Miss Fiona Featherduster's inherited painting. This is a fun lesson in art history, and you will help A. Pintura figure out who painted Miss Featherduster's masterpiece. Compare and contrast Miss Featherduster's painting with works of art by Van Gogh, Raphael, Titian, Millet, Picasso, and Gauguin. By analyzing the color, composition, style and subject, you can help Mr. Pintura figure out the origin of the mystery painting. When you finish this art adventure, go to **Inside Art** for more fun with art history!

Quest questions:

1. What did Miss Fiona Featherduster do for a living?

   _____

2. Who painted *Landscape Near Auvers*?

   _____

3. How many works of art did Picasso produce in his lifetime?

   _____

The Art of Origami

Website:

Joseph Wu's Origami Page

Address:

http://www.origami.vancouver.bc.ca/

Discover the Japanese art of folding paper from this captivating website. Click on **Information**, and then travel through time to **A Brief History of Paper Folding** and learn how origami developed into the amazing art that it is today. The origami tradition was handed down orally from generation to generation for hundreds of years before ever being written. There are many origami diagrams to get you started in this ancient art. Begin with the basics and advance to the model and structural design diagrams. You can also learn about the delicate art of papermaking and the difference between coating paper and wet-folding origami. Follow the link to view an impressive dinosaur skeleton made from wet-folding heavy paper. Don't forget to visit the **Origami Photo Gallery** and watch out for the Chinese water buffalo!

Quest questions:

1. What were the first written instructions for paper folding called?

   _____

2. When and where did paper making originate?

   _____

3. What is the name for machine-made Japanese paper?

   _____

Fun on the Internet

Website:
MaMaMedia

Address:
http://www.mamamedia.com/

Welcome to **MaMaMedia,** a popular Internet site where you can find lots to see, do, and hear. The activities on this site are free, but you must register in order to use them. This site has many areas to explore. Start off by clicking on **Play** and then go to **Surprise!** to play games, make an e-card, or build your own online town. Try *Riddle Machine*, *Kids Web Paint*, and *Cartoon Castles*. Click on **Buzz** to post your work, and see things that other kids have created. Participate in an online poll, and check out the games, riddles, and jokes from the M-gang. One of the best features of **MaMaMedia** is the extensive list of links to other sites, which you can find on the **Romp** page. Finally, go to **Zap** to design your own screen saver. Choose from many different designs and then put it on your screen. An original work of art!

Quest questions:

1. Who are the members of the M-gang?

   _____

2. What do you do in the game *Presto?*

   _____

3. What can you do in **Buzz?**

   _____

The Grammy™ Awards

Website:

The Recording Academy

Address:

http://www.grammy.com/

"Pass the envelope please . . . the Grammy Award goes to . . ." The National Recording Academy, the home of the Grammy Awards, was established to further the cause of musicians and their music. At this site you can search for your favorite musicians and songs and find out if they have been honored by a Grammy Award. You can catch up on what is happening in the music world at the **News Features** section or read about current trends within the music industry at **Arts Watch**. Get involved and vote on controversial issues affecting the recording industry at the **Poll Results** page. Go to the **Forum** to review poll results and read monthly excerpts from *Grammy Magazine*, the Academy's premiere magazine. Visit **Master Track** to find out what music events are taking place in cities across the United States (or in Cyberspace) or check out monthly music events at the **Month at a Glance** page. You can even **Add an Event** to promote music events in your community.

Quest questions:

1. Who can nominate an artist for a Grammy Award?

   _____

2. In what year did Miles Davis win the Lifetime Achievement Award?

   _____

3. Who tallies the votes for the Grammy Awards?

   _____

The Noise of Music

Website:

Energy in the Air:
Sounds from the Orchestra

Address:

http://tqjunior.advanced.org/5116/

Do you hear the wind? You can at this award winning website where you discover that sound is a form of wind energy! The energy is transformed into sound and then recorded. Learn the distinct parts of the orchestral instrument families and then listen to symphonies by Beethoven and Schubert at **The Orchestra**. Explore the differences between noise and music at **Sound is Energy**. Try one of the projects that demonstrates how sound moves in vibrations. Follow the directions to make a drum, bugle, string thing, or a piped instrument on the **Activities** page. This website was designed for *Think Quest Junior*, an annual contest created by Advanced Network and Services, Inc. Advanced Network promotes the development of interactive Internet websites by students around the world. A link to *Think Quest* is provided at this site—check it out!

Quest questions:

1. What four families of instruments make up an orchestra?

   _____

2. What is *frequency*?

   _____

3. Which woodwind instrument is the oldest and dates back as far as 5000 BC?

   _____

Paul Cézanne

Website:
WebMuseum:
Cézanne, Paul

Address:
http://www.oir.ucf.edu/wm/paint/auth/cezanne/

Get to know one of the world's greatest Post-Impressionist painters at this **WebMuseum** site. Cézanne was misunderstood and unappreciated during his lifetime, but has since been called the father of modern painting. Find out why. The site has a detailed biography of Cézanne and looks at the influences in his life that drove him to paint. There is a timeline of the development of his work as well as separate pages for specific paintings. The color images are clear and can be enlarged for a closer look. No games or puzzles, but lots of facts about an amazing artist!

Quest questions:

1. When was Paul Cézanne born?

   _____

2. Where is *Portrait of the Artist's Father* on display?

   _____

3. How big is the Chateau Noir?

   _____

Many people are drawn to a particular kind of entertainment like movies, the outdoors, or video games. Enough knowledge about one of your interests might make you an expert! This is what happens on the World Wide Web. On many websites, the site you are on will provide the names and addresses, or links, to other related sites. Links are usually highlighted in a different color, or are underlined, or both. This is a great way to explore many sites that are all devoted to the same, or related, topics. Pick a topic, explore the sites and their links, and pretty soon you will be an expert, too!

Entertainment

Arnold Schwarzenegger

Website:

Arnold Schwarzenegger

Address:

http://www.schwarzenegger.com

Arnold has become an American hero, proving his versatility and talent by spanning the arenas of acting, physical fitness, and politics. Read his life story, beginning with his childhood in Austria, and learn how he has made it to where he is today. There is a wealth of health and nutrition information in the **Fitness and Nutrition Centers**, where you can learn facts and myths about good health. The movie section is fun, with details on all of Arnold's big screen successes. Take the **Arnold Trivia Challenge** and see how much you know about this amazing man. There are sample video clips, photos, and information on the *Arnold Schwarzenegger Classic*, a "body building event for professionals worldwide."

Quest questions:

1. What was the name of the character that Arnold played in *Kindergarten Cop*?

   _____

2. How old was Arnold when he won the title of Mr. Universe?

   _____

3. What are the names of Arnold's children?

   _____

Dirty Harry: Hero of the Screen

Website:

Clint Eastwood—
The World Wide Web Page

Address:

http://www.clinteastwood.net

This is a wonderful website developed by a clearly devoted fan of Clint Eastwood. There are many audio clips and photographs of this beloved star. There is also an extensive biography tracking Clint's career from the 1950's to the 1990's, with a special section devoted to Clint's stint as the mayor of Carmel. Take one of many trivia tests after you have reviewed the site and see how much you really know about the "Man with No Name." Send an e-postcard with one of several images of Clint to a friend and then vote for your Clint favorites in the **Voting Booth**. Post your questions and comments about Clint on the **Clint Eastwood Bulletin Board** and become a true Clint Eastwood expert.

Quest questions:

1. In which country did Clint film *A Fistful of Dollars*?

_____

2. When was Clint the Mayor of Carmel?

_____

3. What is the name of the TV show Clint appeared in back in the late 1950's?

_____

Fun on the Web

Website:

Squigly's Playhouse

Address:

http//www.squiglysplayhouse.com/

Come to **Squigly's Playhouse** for fun and games on the Web. Choose from games like *picture matches* or *memory*, quizzes on things like pizza toppings, dinosaurs, and game shows, or word scrambles on poisonous plants or purple things. Learn how to make bookends, flowerpots, or a kazoo (among many things) in the **Craft Ideas** section. **Pencil Puzzles** has secret codes, crosswords, and riddles. The **Writing Corner** encourages you to create your own poetry, stories, and book reviews to be posted on the site. Go on to **Jokes and Riddles**, **Brain Teasers**, and **Boredom Busters**! Lot of fun and lots to do! This site is updated every few weeks, so you can come back and play again and again!

Quest questions:

1. How do you get in touch with Squigly?

   _____

2. Has Squigly's Playhouse won the Family Friendly site award?

   _____

3. Are there coloring pages on this site?

   _____

Games
and Fun

Website:

GAMEKIDS—
The International Natural Play Site

Address:

http://www.gamekids.com/

The mission of this site is to encourage kids to "learn and exchange non-computer games and activities." It is written by pre-teens and teens and contains games, activities, artwork, ideas, photographs, recipes, and more. Go to the **Games** page and choose from Easter games, Valentine games, Halloween games, water games, and many more. Visit the **GK Thrift** section with ideas on how to make and save money! The producers of the site encourage their readers to contribute to the site with game and activity ideas. Be sure to visit the **Greeting Card** page, where you can choose from hundreds of topics (send a pizza, say thank you, congratulations, or please write) as well as different backgrounds, text color, greetings and closings, and more.

Quest questions:

1. How do you subscribe to the free online newsletter?

   _____

2. Who writes the content for this site?

   _____

3. Is there a fee to join **GameKids**?

   _____

Hollywood People

Website:

Mr. Showbiz

Address:

http://mrshowbiz.go.com/

Find out everything you ever wanted to know about the rich and famous, the talented and not so talented, and the "who's who" of the entertainment industry. Enter Gwyneth Paltrow's name into the search field and you will instantly come up with over 600 results. Go to **News**, **Movies**, **TV**, **Features**, **Games**, **Music**, or **Celebrities** and get the latest on your favorites. There is also plenty of movie history and star biography information here, so dig in and get the dirt you are after!

Quest questions:

1. In what year did Tom Cruise star in *Born on the Fourth of July?*

   _____

2. When was Jennifer Love Hewitt born?

   _____

3. What is the name of the Cowboy Junkies' 1996 album?

   _____

The Making of a Documentary

Website:

NOVA Online—Avalanche!

Address:

http://www.pbs.org/wgbh/nova/avalanche/

How do people make documentaries of natural phenomena like avalanches? Are they simply at the right place at the right time? Find out how a cinematographer captures an avalanche on film and the planning and hazards that go along with his or her job. View avalanche clips at the bottom of the page. Find out what makes an avalanche occur and how you can use *snow sense* to avoid being trapped in one. The story behind how this film was made is thrilling, and filled with excitement and frustration. Read about the people involved in the lengthy process of making this film, a process that took place over a year's time and included trips to Colorado, Montana, and Switzerland.

Quest questions:

1. What is a "crash box"?

_____

2. What is a "fire in the hole"?

_____

3. Who is Beth Hoppe?

_____

MTV™ Backstage

Website:

MTV™ Online

Address:

http://www.mtv.com/

Wow! We are jammin' at this cool website! Click on **Bands a-z** to unearth a listing from A-Z of all the bands ever to appear on MTV. You can even download and watch MTV exclusive on-line videos. Test your knowledge about your favorite bands at the **Music** page. Go to the **Movie Awards** page to see the winners of the off-the-wall video categories. You can check out the latest music happenings and read interviews with your favorite band members at the **News** page. You can also view the current top 10 singles and top 20 selling albums along with your own local area charts. Go to the **Chat Room** to find out when your favorite band is going to be interviewed. Send in your questions and you just may get to chat with them. Check out the interview archives to read past online chat sessions with big name bands.

Quest questions:

1. What is Howie's (from the Back Street Boys) favorite sport?

   _____

2. What former Beatle invited Hanson to appear in his music video?

   _____

3. What is the current #1 single?

   _____

Nintendo™ Rules!

Website:

The Official Home Page for Nintendo™

Address:

http://www.nintendo.com/home/index.html

Everything you could ever want to know about Nintendo, the games and the company, can be found at this site. There are separate pages for Nintendo 64, Game Boy, and Super NES with in-depth descriptions and photos of the games. Go to the **Code Bank** to get "the best codes for all games" in a massive database. This is a great feature if a game has become frustrating. **NSIDER** has bulletin boards and chat rooms, as well as articles, contests, and games like **Pokémon Scramble** and **Nintendo Sports Crossword**. The games are great because they do not have too many graphics and are easily downloaded. The **Consumer Service** page is helpful for technical questions and you can even e-mail Nintendo directly if you have a question. **Corporate Info** tells the Nintendo story, beginning in the late 1800's, and **Company Connection** provides links to international Nintendo sites.

Quest questions:

1. Which city is the home base of Nintendo?

_____

2. What is "Hanafuda"?

_____

3. How many countries have their own Nintendo sites listed as links?

_____

The Oscars^{SM}

Website:

Welcome to the Academy of
Motion Picture Arts and Sciences

Address:

http://www.oscars.org/

Want to be a star? On this web page you can find out all about the upcoming and recent Academy Awards. Today the Academy has over 6,000 members and membership is limited to invitation only by the Board of Governors. Click on **Academy Awards** to learn all about the history of this spectacular event. Visit *The Oscar and Other Academy Awards* to learn about the Award statuette. The Academy of Motion Picture Arts and Sciences, established in 1927 with 36 members, promotes the art of filmmaking. Take a tour of the **Center For Motion Picture Study**. Don't forget to search the database to see if your favorite films received any awards or nominations!

Quest questions:

1. What is the official name of the Oscar statuette?

   _____

2. What is the Oscar statuette made of?

   _____

3. What is the Oscar a sculpture of?

   _____

Ride a
Roller Coaster

Website:

Ultimate Roller Coaster -
Roller Coasters, Theme Parks,
and Thrill Rides

Address:

http://www.ultimaterollercoaster.com/

Climb up and strap in for a wild ride at this fast-paced, thrill-seeking website. Get in line for **Featured Rollercoaster** to explore coasters like the *Canyon Blaster Coaster*, which is indoors in Las Vegas, to the *Batman the Ride* coaster in Atlanta, where your feet dangle freely in the air. Read about the novel thrill rides coming soon to a park near you on the **New** page or check out all of the things happening inside theme parks at **News and Rumors**. View the gravity defying twists and turns of some wild coasters in the **Picture Gallery** and stop over in the **Record Book** to find out how the different coasters match up. Search the **Roller Coaster Yellow Pages** for information about any amusement park in the U.S. and get ready to plan your next ride!

Quest questions:

1. What is the fastest running roller coaster in the U.S. today?

_____

2. How long is the longest wooden roller coaster?

_____

3. In what year was the steepest drop wooden coaster built?

_____

Just like your body needs food to make it work and function, many websites require you to provide a password in order to explore their site. The site will not function or work for you if you do not "feed" it the right information. The people who design websites do this for several reasons. They want to make sure you are who you say you are, kind of like a security check. They also want to keep track of your participation on the site, like if you are playing an ongoing game and the site is keeping track of your scores. When you make up a password, try to think of a password that will be easy for you to remember (like a favorite character from a story) but hard for a stranger to figure out. Be sure to write it down somewhere, just in case you forget. Many sites have a way for you to contact them if you *do* forget your password.

Food

Cooking for Kids

Website:

Jell-O™ Kid's Cooking Fun

Address:

http://www.kraftfoods.com/html/features/jello.html

If you don't know your way around the kitchen, its time you start learning. If you are a good cook, you might want to try some new recipes. You can learn all about cooking at this wonderful website designed by Kraft foods, especially for kids. First, read over **Cooking Tips** to learn exactly how to boil water and the different ways of measuring liquids and dry items. Check out **Equipment** and see pictures of different cooking tools, like a wire whisk and a teaspoon. **Cooking Words** teaches you recipe language, like the difference between "beat" and "stir." Now, put on your chef's hat and click on a recipe to travel further into the Kraft cookbook.

Quest questions:

1. What does "thaw" mean?

   _____

2. What makes Jell-O become solid?

   _____

3. What is a wire whisk?

   _____

Ice Cream
for the People

Website:

Welcome to B & J's™ International

Address:

http://www.benandjerrys.com

Who doesn't love ice cream? Ben and Jerry's have put together a delicious website full of facts and trivia on the yummy cold stuff and on their unique business approach. Read about the **Factory Tours**, send e-cards to friends, and get the scoop on all your favorite flavors of ice cream. Visit the **Flavor Graveyard** to find out which flavors didn't make the cut, and find out the address of the scoop shop closest to you. In honor of the company's anniversary, the owners designate one day each year as Free Cone Day—they give out free cones all day long! Find out when the next Free Cone Day is. There are games to play and puzzles to solve, and a research site about the company. Read about the owners' concerns about the environment and their generous contributions to the community. This website is updated frequently and is well-designed. A great company with a great product!

Quest questions:

1. From which college did Jerry Greenfield graduate?

   _____

2. What is the address of the only Scoop Shop in Louisiana?

   _____

3. How much would you have to pay for a Ben and Jerry's ice cream scoop ordered over the Internet?

   _____

Jelly Beans!

Website:

Jelly Belly™ Online

Address:

http://www.jellybelly.com/

Jelly beans are not just for Easter anymore! This website brings these wonderful little beans to you in a fun and intriguing way. Did you know that the two Jelly Belly factories in the U.S. can produce 100,000 pounds of jelly beans each day? Or that Ronald Reagan was such a fan of Jelly Bellies that 3½ tons of red, white, and blue beans were shipped to the Presidential Inaugural Ceremonies in January of 1981? Learn all about the amazing Jelly Belly at the **Q & A**, **History**, and **Factory Tour** pages. You can also register to receive free Jelly Belly samples! Be sure to check out the **Art Gallery** where the Statue of Liberty, Abraham Lincoln, and Amelia Earhart (to name just a few) are all immortalized in Jelly Bellies.

Quest questions:

1. When did the Herman Goelitz factory begin making special jelly beans?

   _____

2. When can you take a tour of the Jelly Belly Factory?

   _____

3. How many calories are in a single Jelly Belly?

   _____

Yummy Candy

Website:

Welcome to KidsCandy!!!

Address:

http://www.kidscandy.org/

Sponsored by the National Confectioners Association and the Chocolate Manufacturers Association, this site appeals to the candy lover in all of us. Test your knowledge of candy in the *Sweet Stuff* quiz and see if you can answer questions like: "How much candy do Americans consume in one year?" **Kids in the Kitchen** has recipes for making Candy Chipmunks and Chocolate Covered Words, and **Brain Candy** gives you facts about candy and the histories of chocolate, the candy bar, candy canes, and jelly beans. There are links to other candy sites, such as Hershey, M & M's, and Snickers. There is also a link to *Candy Time*, another site devoted entirely to sweets.

Quest questions:

1. How many glasses of chocolate did Montezuma, the Aztec Emperor of Mexico, drink every day?

   _____

2. What country has the highest per capita consumption of candy in the world?

   _____

3. Is powdered sugar one of the ingredients in rock candy?

   _____

When you need information, you often need to explore multiple resources in order to get what you are looking for. For example, if you are trying to find a particular Pokémon card, you will need to ask friends for trades, call a store that carries Pokémon cards, or check on the Internet. When you are trying to find something on the Internet, there are many different sources for acquiring information. These sites are called "search engines." A search engine will take the word that you type in and then give you a list and very brief description of sites that might interest you. Metacrawler, Lycos, Excite, Yahoo, and Alta Vista are examples of search engines. Try them all and see which one you like the best.

FYI

Answers to Just About Everything

Website:

Welcome to How Stuff Works

Address:

http://www.howstuffworks.com/

You could spend days at this website discovering amazing things about how stuff works—cool stuff you may wonder about but aren't taught in school! Learn about things as small as a cellular phone to things as large as a cruise missile. At **How Time Works** discover how the calendar months were named, that July and August are named after Roman Emperors, and that Augustus borrowed a day from February so that his month would have the same amount of days as July. Take a peek at **Things Around the House** to view the insides of gadgets around the house. Find out that the red eye in some of your pictures is really a reflection of the blood vessels nourishing the retina. Check out the **Question of the Day** to learn interesting things like how ice is made for an ice rink. You can also submit questions to be answered and then sign up for the *How Stuff Works Newsletter* to receive new articles published every week. All you need is an e-mail address!

Quest questions:

1. What direction do 99% of all tornadoes rotate?

   _____

2. How many gallons of gas can a 747 hold?

   _____

3. How much oxygen does one person use in a day?

   _____

For Your Health

Website:

KidsHealth.org—
Calling All Kids!

Address:

http://www.kidshealth.org/kid/index.html

Welcome to **Kid's Health**, where you can find out all you need to know about being healthy. Come and read articles like *Are You Shy? Find Out Why* and *Am I Too Fat or Too Thin?* At the **Staying Healthy** page there are articles like *Being Good to Your Body* and *Keeping Fit and Having Fun.* There are even kid-tested health recipes for better nutrition. Visit the **My Body** page to learn how your body works and read about the different parts of the body. In the **Kids Only Closet** there are games to play and activities such as trying to find out what bug just bit you. Steady your hands at the **Dissect a Frog** page, where you can virtually dissect a frog. In **Kids' Talk** you can find out the answers to questions asked by kids just like you. You can also find out why the doctor examines you during a checkup and discover facts about the medicines that make you feel better. At the **Word** page you can browse through a dictionary of medical terms just for kids.

Quest questions:

1. Is your pulse felt on an artery or on a vein?

   _____

2. What vital thing needed by all organs is carried by red blood cells?

   _____

3. What does a stethoscope magnify?

   _____

Questions, Questions

Website:

Ask Jeeves™ for Kids

Address:

http://www.ajkids.com/

This is an excellent site to begin a search for information and is a nice child-friendly alternative to the huge search engines. **Ask Jeeves** encourages you to ask a question about any topic. Once you have submitted your question, for example, "Why is the sky blue?", the database comes back with questions to help you narrow down your topic. After you have answered the more specific questions, you are then sent to a child-safe site that can answer the question you have submitted. The **Student Resources** page can help you find topics that interest you, and the **Teacher Resources** page is great place for adults to get new ideas. When you click on **Today's Word** you will be sent to the Infoplease.com site, where a word will be used in a sentence and you get to choose from a list of four definitions to find the correct one. It is a fun way to learn a new word! Take the **Solar Eclipse Tour** and get answers to questions such as "Why does a solar eclipse happen?" and "Where can I find myths about the sun?" Before you leave, send an e-card to a friend and pass along the address for **Ask Jeeves**!

Quest questions:

1. What are teeth made out of?

   _____

2. Who was the 21st President of the United States?

   _____

3. What are the three longest rivers in the world?

   _____

Stocks, Bonds, and Investing

Website:
The Young Investor Website

Address:
http://www.younginvestor.com/pick.shtml

It is never too early to start planning for your future, whether you want to save for a new bike or save for college. Created by Fidelity, one of the largest financial institutions in the world, this site provides anything you want to know about saving money. Pick your own guide based upon your own saving personality or style. Read the six bios and choose a guide from characters like the socially conscientious Planet Lisa to the conservative Webster. Once you have chosen your guide and entered the site, click on *See how you measure up* to test your knowledge of money, saving and investing. Visit the **Library** to learn *Money Basics*, tips on *General Investing*, the answers to some *Frequently Asked Questions*, or look up money terms in the *Dictionary*. In the **Game Room** play *Money-Tration*, a money fact memory game, or the *Young Investor Trivia Game* to see how much you know about Wall Street. Don't forget to try a few **Brain Teasers**. You can send in and read answers to questions at **Mr. Tightwad**.

Quest questions:

1. What is an income tax?

_____

2. What does it mean if you own a share of stock in a company?

_____

3. What is a Bull market? A Bear market?

_____

Tobacco Road

Website:

CDC's TIPS—TIPS 4 Kids

Address:

http://www.cdc.gov/nccdphp/osh/tipskids.htm

Discover the truth about tobacco and its harmful effects on your body at this health-oriented information site from the Center for Disease Control. Start off with **What You(th) Should Know about Tobacco** for basic facts on tobacco and how it hinders athletic performance and appearance. Read about what Christy Turlington and Boyz II Men think about smoking and what their reasons are for just saying no. Go to the **Surgeon General's** page and read the *Real Deal about Tobacco* to get some straight answers. Check out **Up in Smoke** to see what a waste of money tobacco can be. Take the quiz and see how well you understand the dangers of tobacco use. After you complete the quiz, CDC will send you a free poster. Go to **You Smoke, You Choke** to see original artwork by students in Arizona and explore other links provided by this site. Many teens consider tobacco use every day—make an informed decision and stay healthy!

Quest questions:

1. What does nicotine do to your blood vessels?

   _____

2. Approximately how many adolescents in the United States smoke cigarettes?

   _____

3. When do most people begin smoking?

   _____

World News for Kids

Website:

Junior Scholastic Online

Address:

http://www.scholastic.com/kids/

Catch up on world events and investigate the news kid-style from **Junior Scholastic Online**. Go to **News Zone** to read late-breaking, up-to-the-minute news from around the globe. Hop over to **Research Tools** to dig out past news articles. Do you think you are informed on current world issues? Test yourself by trying the **News Challenge**. Follow the clues in the *Map Man Game* to test your knowledge of geography—the clues are posted all week and can pinpoint a geographical area as large as a continent or as small as a lake. The **Web Connect** page provides links to all of the websites that deal with current world issues. Get involved and vote in the current Junior Scholastic poll at **Debate It**.

Quest questions:

1. Who invented basketball?

   _____

2. Has violent crime by juveniles increased or decreased in the last 10 years?

   _____

3. Yugoslavia broke apart because of the collapse of what form of government?

   _____

Where Are They Now?

Website:

Find a Grave

Address:

http://www.findagrave.com/

A strange idea, but a fascinating site. Look up the final resting places of the signers of the Declaration of Independence, Lucille Ball, Mickey Mantle, and almost anyone else you can think of. Search by name, location, or claim to fame. There is almost always a little biographical information, including cause of death. Many of the entries have a photograph of the gravesite, along with a map of the spot. Go to **Posthumous Reunions** and find out where Bonnie and Clyde, the cast of *I Love Lucy*, the Kennedy Family, and others are buried. Find information on cemeteries, celebrity death, and other related topics under **Links and Accolades**. This is also a good site to check out if you are not sure about an individual's current status; is he dead or still alive? Believe it or not, it is hard to tear yourself away from this historical site.

Quest questions:

1. Who was Mary Lyon and where is she buried?

   _____

2. How did Charles Pinkey die?

   _____

3. Who was James Pierpont?

   _____

Yahooligans!™

Website:

Yahooligans!™

Address:

http://www.yahooligans.com/

Yahooligans is an index of the Internet designed for web surfers ages 7–12; and what an index it is! There are two ways to begin with **Yahooligans**. First, if you know the subject matter in which you are interested, enter the topic in the *Search* field at the top of the **Home** page. That will send you on your way. Or, if you want to surf a bit, choose from one of the general topics listed on the **Home** page: **Around the World**, **Arts and Entertainment**, **Computers and Games**, **School Bell**, **Science and Nature**, or **Sports and Recreation**. Within each category are lists of subcategories. Each subcategory contains even more categories. For instance, start with **School Bell**. Then go to *Language Arts*, then to *Authors*. There are over two hundred links just for the topic *Authors*. Another resource in Yahooligans is under the **Help** page, under *FAQ* (Frequently Asked Questions). There is a good introduction to the Internet, with three levels of quizzes that you can take to test your Internet knowledge. This is a wonderful, basic site to get started exploring the Web.

Quest questions:

1. What is ftp?

   _____

2. What is Claire Danes' middle name?

   _____

3. Name three roller coasters located at Paramount's Great America Park in Santa Clara, CA.

   _____

Traveling to new and different places can be both exciting and fun, but in order for the trip to be a success, you need to have a map to show you where you are going and the best way to get there. Think of your browser as your map, or tool, to connect you to where you want to go on the World Wide Web. The two most popular browsers are Netscape Navigator and Microsoft Explorer, both of which are very easy to use. Have a good trip!

Geography and Travel

America the Great

Website:

50 States and Capitals

Address:

http://www.50states.com/

This well-organized website has oodles of fun facts about each and every state in The United States of America, including all of the commonwealths and territories. There is information on population, industry, tourism, state flags, and weather. For those of you who like to plan ahead, click on the **Colleges and University Directory** to find links to private and public universities, as well as community and technical colleges within a state. The **Community Pages Directory** lists the communities within the state and provides links to the communities online. Explore the **Alphabetical List of Nations** where all the countries in the world are listed. Click on a country to read about their economy, people, and the local news. Find a picture of the country's flag and local maps, listen to their national anthem, or find out about the current weather conditions within the country. AMAZING! You can also access over 10,000 websites from **50states.com**!

Quest questions:

1. What are the two most populated countries on earth?

   _____

2. What was the first constitutionally declared state in the US?

   _____

3. What is smallest state in the US at 1,231 square miles? Compare that to the largest state at 615,230 sq. miles.

   _____

Explore Antarctica

Website:

Glacier

Address:

http://www.glacier.rice.edu/

Go on an expedition into the land of glaciers and visit this website that explores Antarctica, home to 70% of the Earth's water supply. Come and learn how subtle warming of the climate in Antarctica can effect the rest of the world by substantially raising the sea levels. Go through the **Introduction** to learn about the seasons and types of ice and in *Picture This* you can browse a photo journal of the continent. Visit the **Expedition** section to learn about who travels to Antarctica, and what it is like to live and work in such a cold and remote environment. Meet the scientists who live and work on the continent and discover how difficult it is to get there. Travel with them on their research vessels as they search for distant ice shelves. At the **Oceans** page you can learn all about Oceanography and discover how the oceans are all connected to become one big ocean.

Quest questions:

1. Do polar bears live in Antarctica?

   _____

2. How much precipitation falls in Antarctica each year?

   _____

3. How much of Antarctica is covered with ice?

   _____

Investigate the Loch Ness Monster

Website:

Official Loch Ness Monster
Exhibition/Nessie on the Net
in Scotland!

Address:

http://www.lochness.co.uk/

Explore the fascinating Scottish Highlands and catch a glimpse of the Loch Ness Monster's habitat at this incredible website. Begin by touring the **The Official Loch Ness Monster Exhibition Site** that moves you "through 500 million years in 40 minutes." Learn the interesting history of the Great Glen and how, although it is millions of years old, it is the most active earthquake zone in the UK. Visit **Nessie on the Net** to view live pictures of the lake and start your own search for the Loch Ness Monster. Watch videos of witnesses telling their stories of sightings! Find out when Nessie was last spotted. If you follow the link to the **Highland Games** you can learn all about this Scottish competitive tradition that has gone on for years and years.

Quest questions:

1. Because of its unique position to cross winds, how high can under-water waves in Lake Loch Ness reach?

    _____

2. Who first started reporting stories of a monster in Loch Ness?

    _____

3. What is the "tossing the caber" event in the Highland Games?

    _____

Learn a Language

Website:

Foreign Languages
for Travelers

Address:

http://www.travlang.com/languages/

Sprechen sie Deutsch? Parlez-vous Français? Anata wa Nihongo go wo hanasemasuka? Parla Italiano? Do you speak German? French? Japanese? Italian? At this wonderful website you can learn **Basic Words**, **Numbers**, **Shopping and Dining** phrases, **Travel, Directions, Places**, and **Times and Dates** for over 70 languages from countries around the world from Albania to Zulu. There is even a spell check available in 33 languages. Amaze your friends and learn new words from different languages each week. Be sure to check out the similarities in several of the languages.

Quest questions:

1. How do you say "I do not understand" in Italian?

   _____

2. How do you say "I'll buy it" in French?

   _____

3. How do you ask "Where is the bathroom?" in Spanish?

   _____

Map the World

Website:
Welcome to
MapQuest

Address:
http://www.mapquest.com/

Are you lost? You won't be for long at this website. MapQuest is a comprehensive interactive atlas that can be used for long distance travel plans or locating directions to a friend's party. Print maps of cities and countries around the world, or of specific destinations by typing in the address or zip code. Go to the **Driving Directions** page to find specific directions between addresses or cities. There is even a travel guide and planner where you can learn all about a city and its attractions, and find out the weather forecast. If you need a topographic map you can order it from the comprehensive **Map Store**. Join **My Map Quest** and instantly pull up directions from favorite destinations!

Quest questions:

1. How many estimated driving miles is it from the city of Los Angeles, CA to New York, NY?

   _____

2. Is it shorter to drive from Denver to San Francisco or from Denver to Chicago?

   _____

3. How far is it from your house to the White House at 1600 Pennsylvania Avenue, Washington DC?

   _____

The Peace Corps

Website:

Peace Corps
Kids World

Address:

http://www.peacecorps.gov/kids/

Make a difference is the theme of the Peace Corps and this website shows how thousands of American volunteers have done just that. Find out what countries the Peace Corps serves, the kind of work that Peace Corps volunteers do, and the benefits of becoming a Peace Corps volunteer, or another kind of volunteer. Read about the history of the Peace Corps, the goals of the Corps, and what it means to be a Peace Corps volunteer. Find out how kids around the world are making a difference in their own communities and how you can make a difference in yours. Go to **Explore the World** for detailed information on some of the countries where Peace Corps volunteers serve. **Food, Friends, and Fun** introduces you to holidays, food, schools and recreation in different parts of the world. You can even send a postcard to a friend and tell him or her what you've learned. Play **Pack Your Bags** to test your knowledge of what being a Peace Corps volunteer entails. **Tell Me a Story** posts a folk tale from a different part of the world.

Quest questions:

1. Who founded the Peace Corps?

   _____

2. How old must you be to join the Peace Corps?

   _____

3. In what year was the first Peace Corps volunteer elected to U.S. Congress?

   _____

Pharaohs and Pyramids

Website:

Little Horus website

Address:

http://www.horus.ics.org.eg/

Meet Little Horus, the animated bird from Egypt, and explore the first Egyptian website for children. Check out the interesting places to visit in Egypt, learn about 7,000 years of Egyptian history and civilization, and make friends from around the world when you join Little Horus' Club. Learn Arabic symbols and numbers when you go to **Horus' Club**, and design your own homepage there. Facts about Egyptian culture, economy, and holidays as well as photographs and maps help illustrate the site. The **Entertainment** page has games, coloring pages, quizzes, recipes and contests. You can also translate your name from English to Hieroglyphics! Click on Arabic or French to see the site in the two languages used most often in Egypt. This site is updated weekly, so check back often to see what's new.

Quest questions:

1. What is the name of the First Lady of Egypt?

   _____

2. How many days did it take to dry out a body for mummification?

   _____

3. When did Napoleon Bonaparte come to Egypt?

   _____

Safe Spelunking

Website:

The United States
Show Cave Directory

Address:

http://www.goodearthgraphics.com/showcave.html

Get ready to go spelunking into some of the most fascinating caves on Earth and take a peek at some amazing rock and mineral formations. Visit the **Virtual Cave** page to view pictures and read descriptions of more than 40 types of mineral deposits and formations that can be found in caves. Be sure to click on the *Cave Image Map* to view a map of where the unique formations would be positioned in a real cave. Visit the **U.S. Show Caves Directory** to find out about caves that are open for public access in your area, and follow the direct links to caves that host a web page. If you are planning a trip to a real cave, check out the **Cave Photography Tips** page.

Quest questions:

1. Where is America's highest underground waterfall?

   _____

2. In what shape do stalactites form?

   _____

3. What is the world's longest cave?

   _____

Sky Scrapers

Website:

World's
Tallest Buildings

Address:

http://www.worldstallest.com/

Get ready to scale the tallest buildings in the world! Once you reach the top, start your tour on the **97th floor**, where you find out about buildings that are under construction, on hold, or that were proposed but never built, like the mile-high Illinois building. The **96th floor** will take you to WTB magazine for interesting articles about the world's tallest buildings. On the **95th floor** there are links that describe the architecture, and the building process involved in making skyscrapers structurally sound. Be sure to check out the web cams and the views from observatories on the **94th floor**. The **93rd floor** provides a list of all the buildings in the world that are over 1000 feet tall. On the **44th floor** you can send questions and find answers posted from the author. When you stop on the **Ground Floor** you can read all of the latest news on the **World's Tallest Buildings**.

Quest questions:

1. What is the tallest building in the world?

   _____

2. What famous architect proposed and created plans for the mile-high Illinois building, which was never built?

   _____

3. What building houses the highest occupied floor?

   _____

South Dakota

Website:

A Guide to the
Great Sioux Nation

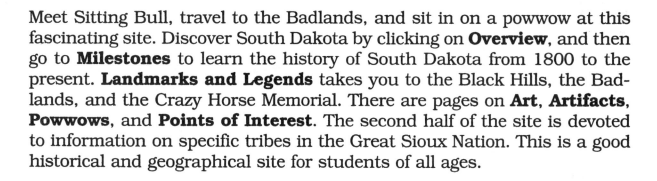

Address:

http://www.state.sd.us/state/executive/tourism/sioux/sioux.htm

Meet Sitting Bull, travel to the Badlands, and sit in on a powwow at this fascinating site. Discover South Dakota by clicking on **Overview**, and then go to **Milestones** to learn the history of South Dakota from 1800 to the present. **Landmarks and Legends** takes you to the Black Hills, the Badlands, and the Crazy Horse Memorial. There are pages on **Art**, **Artifacts**, **Powwows**, and **Points of Interest**. The second half of the site is devoted to information on specific tribes in the Great Sioux Nation. This is a good historical and geographical site for students of all ages.

Quest questions:

1. When did the United States purchase the Louisiana territory from France?

   _____

2. How big is the Badlands National Park?

   _____

3. What is the language of the Sisseton-Wahpeton Dakota Nation?

   _____

Tower
of
London

Website:

The Tower of London
KIDS Tour

Address:

http://www.toweroflondontour.com/kids/

Go along with Reginald Raven as he takes you on a tour of his home, the Tower of London. View photographs of the Tower Bridge and the River Thames as you begin the tour, and then go on to read about William the Conqueror, who built the castle over 1,000 years ago. The tour continues with lots of historical information, including details about the infamous Henry VIII. View photographs of Beefeaters, read about the Great Fire of London, and the origins behind Guy Fawkes Day. The tour has audio to accompany it and includes the sound of fireworks and the squawking of the ravens. Conclude your visit at the White Tower and then take the quiz to see how much you learned on the tour. There is also a maze and a place to send a musical postcard, as well as a good list of other kids' links.

Quest questions:

1. Which visitors does Reginald like best?

   _____

2. What is a raven's favorite food?

   _____

3. Who was King Henry VIII's oldest daughter?

   _____

The World's Most Incredible Places

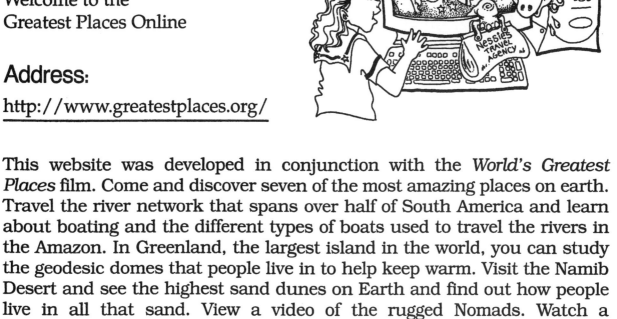

Website:

Welcome to the
Greatest Places Online

Address:

http://www.greatestplaces.org/

This website was developed in conjunction with the *World's Greatest Places* film. Come and discover seven of the most amazing places on earth. Travel the river network that spans over half of South America and learn about boating and the different types of boats used to travel the rivers in the Amazon. In Greenland, the largest island in the world, you can study the geodesic domes that people live in to help keep warm. Visit the Namib Desert and see the highest sand dunes on Earth and find out how people live in all that sand. View a video of the rugged Nomads. Watch a chameleon in action or listen to the lemur call in Madagascar. Learn about the magnificent rainbows created at Iguazu Falls and learn how to do erosion activities in your own yard. View pictures and read about the amazing Tibetan monasteries. On the **Activities** page you will find directions to making a *Madagascar Solitaire Game* from a sand and starch mixture, or join in the *Greatest Places Online Discussions*.

Quest questions:

1. What is the key to survival for the Nomads on the Tibetan Plateau?

   _____

2. In what country are the Iguazu Falls?

   _____

3. What was the first paper, found in the Okavango Delta, made of?

   _____

The Internet is not governed or monitored by one source. Not only should you abide by security standards, but you should also pay careful attention to your "netiquette" — your online manners. You can communicate with friends by sending written messages through e-mail, instant messaging, and in chat rooms, but be sure to choose your words carefully. You may think what you have written is funny, but your friends may not read it that way. Since they can't see you that you are smiling, they may falsely interpret your message and become offended.

History and Government

All About Money

Website:
Welcome to the
US Treasury Department

Address:
http://www.ustreas.gov/

Time is money, so be sure to spend some time learning about the US monetary system and how it works at the **US Department of Treasury Official Website**. Take a virtual tour of Washington DC's third oldest federally occupied building and view the **Cash Room** and the *Burglar Proof Vault*. Enter the **Learning Vault** to explore the duties and functions of the Treasury Department and find out about coins, paper currency, the tax system, and the US budget and debt. Visit the **Treasury for Kid's** page to learn the subtle design features that can help you detect fake money and learn what to do if it ends up in your hands. Visit **Play the Game** and go to the **Bureau of Engraving and Printing's Games** to play *Count the Cash* and practice processing money or *Face Flips* to match faces to the notes on which they belong.

Quest questions:

1. What is the largest note that has ever been printed?

   _____

2. The US Mint produces an average of how many coins per day?

   _____

3. What does the eye in the pyramid on the back of the one-dollar bill stand for?

   _____

The British Monarchy

Website:

The British Monarchy:
The Official Website

Address:

http://www.royal.gov.uk/index.htm

Stroll down the red carpet and get a glimpse of the spectacular lifestyle and personalities behind the throne of England. Come explore the many facets of the Monarchy and its long-lasting reign over England. Visit **Today's Royal Family** to read official biographies of the Queen, The Queen Mother, The Prince of Wales, The Duke of York, Prince Edward, and more. Learn all about the life and death of Princess Diana. Delve into the rich history and architectural style at the **Royal Palaces** page or examine the origins on the Monarchy, the oldest form of government on earth, at **Monarchy Through the Ages**. Visit the **Royal Collection** to learn about the thousands of pieces of arts, jewels, and treasures held by the Queen of England and discover the splendor that surrounds the transfer of power at the **Accession, Coronation, and Succession** page.

Quest questions:

1. Who was the last monarch to pawn the Crown Jewels?

   _____

2. Who was the last King to lead his men into battle?

   _____

3. What is the British Flag called?

   _____

Early American Pioneers

Website:

Pioneers

Address:

http://tqjunior.advanced.org/6400/

Explore life with the early American pioneers at this kid-produced site. Well-written, well-researched, and easy to navigate, learning about the pioneers has never been this much fun! Research questions such as **Who were the pioneers?** and **What are some of the trails they used?** Within the answers to these questions are links to other interesting facts including a glossary of terms and maps showing the routes that pioneers took. Learn about life on the trail and explore topics like fire building, crossing the rivers, pioneer toys, and the dangers that pioneers faced. Help decide what a pioneer family should take on the trail with them, based upon the weight of each item. Activities include a word find, several quizzes, and directions on how to make a buzzsaw or a corn husk doll. Be sure to read about the nine and ten-year-old authors of this site, who put the site together for the ThinkQuest competition. Listen to pioneer music like *Sweet Betsy From Pike* and *Buffalo Gals*, try out pioneer recipes, and meet the real pioneer family that inspired the website.

Quest questions:

1. What is "homesteading"?

   _____

2. Who led the wagon trail?

   _____

3. Who is Maurine Walpole Liles?

   _____

Famous Explorers

Website:

Explorers of
the World

Address:

http://www.bham.wednet.edu/explore.htm

Come meet and learn about the many individuals who have gone forth and
explored the world to do new and different things. Produced by the Bellingham Public School system in Bellingham, WA, this site is divided into four
different topics—Explorers of **Land**, **Ideas**, **Sky**, and **Art**. Each section has
links to individual biographies of great explorers. Read about Captain
James Cook, the English explorer, Alexander Graham Bell, the inventor of
the telephone, Sally Ride, the first woman in space, and Mary Cassat, the
Impressionist painter. Find out what the ten characteristics of a *Profile of
Greatness* are and what kinds of people choose a life of exploration and
discovery. Do some exploring yourself, and follow the links to other good
biography sites.

Quest questions:

1. How much did Susan B. Anthony earn as a teacher in 1846?

   _____

2. How many children does Stephen Hawking have?

   _____

3. What is the name of the airplane that Charles Lindbergh flew
   across the ocean?

   _____

Fly with the Blue Angels

Website:

The United States Navy Blue Angels

Address:

http://www.blueangels.navy.mil/

Soar through the skies with the Blue Angels as they perform daring acrobatics in air shows around the United States. Meet the "Boss," a former accountant, and the other men behind the throttle of the amazing aircraft. Read the biographies of the pilots to find out how they became Blue Angels. Learn about the marine crew that supports the Blue Angels with their *Fat Albert Airlines*. Check out the **Squadron History** of the Blue Angels, learn how they got started, and read about the different types of aircraft they have flown over the years. Check out the **Show Schedule** page to view the itinerary of the Blue Angels air shows and locate a show in your area. Join the other 300 million people who have witnessed their gravity defying stunts since 1946.

Quest questions:

1. How many flight hours do you need to be "Boss" of the Blue Angels?

   _____

2. What is "Fat Albert"?

   _____

3. How many miles do the Blue Angels fly every year?

   _____

The Lewis and Clark Expedition

Website:

Discovering Lewis and Clark

Address:

http://www.lewis-clark.org/

Pack your imaginary bags and travel back in time to June 20, 1803. Travel and explore wild uncharted territory west of the Missouri River with Lewis and Clark as they go on their famous and historic expedition. This website combines a narrative of the journey along with pictures from the era and maps of their trek through the frontier in search of a trading river route to the Pacific Ocean. Be sure to check out the fascinating journal entries and note William Clark's creative spelling entries—he felt that a man of little intelligence would spell a word only one way.

Quest questions:

1. What did President Thomas Jefferson call the Lewis and Clark Expedition?

   _____

2. How many states were in the United States of America at the time of the expedition?

   _____

3. What was the ultimate purpose of the expedition?

   _____

Meet Anne Frank

Website:

Anne Frank Online

Address:

http://www.annefrank.com/

Anne Frank's Diary has been translated into over 50 languages and is one of the most widely read books in the world. It has crossed continents and cultures to teach other generations about the evils of mankind, with the hope of preventing future crimes against humanity. This website is dedicated to providing information about Anne Frank, her family, and her diary. Click on **Anne Frank: Her Life and Times** to learn a short history of her life before the war, how her family fled Germany for Holland, and how her family lived in hiding, but was captured and then sent to concentration camps. Learn that Anne's parents gave her a diary for her birthday shortly before the family escaped the German Army and how she filled that diary with her thoughts and concerns while in hiding. Come and learn about the heroic efforts of a few individuals to save the diary and the determined dedication of Anne's father to have her story told.

Quest questions:

1. How long did Anne Frank and her family live in hiding in the secret annex?

   _____

2. Who rescued Anne's diary after the family was captured?

   _____

3. How many of the seven hiding in the secret annex survived the concentration camps?

   _____

The Titanic in Cyberspace

Website:

Titanic. Destination . . . *Cyberspace.*

Address:

http://www.gwi.net/~paul/

We all know how the story ends, but this site gives a good background of the mighty Titanic and the events that led up to the ship sinking to the bottom of the ocean. Read the shortened version of the Titanic's story and then view photos and read quotes from some of the ship's passengers. The stories they tell are incredible. Go to the **Links** page for other photo sites of the Titanic, as well as sites with greater detail about the ship and her first and only voyage.

Quest questions:

1. How many passengers were on the Titanic?

   _____

2. What was the name of the Chief Officer aboard the Titanic?

   _____

3. What was the name of the rescue ship that arrived early Monday morning?

   _____

Visit a Viking Ship

Website:

Gaia Home Page

Address:

http://home.c2i.net/hovla/gaia/index.html

If you have ever wondered what it was like to sail on a Viking ship, this site is for you. Learn the history of the Gokstad ship, where it was discovered, when it was built, and what its purpose was. Meet the crew of the rebuilt ship named Gaia, view photographs of the restoration, and get Viking ship sailing tips. There are pages on boat building, Viking trade, and specs for the Gaia. The site is written by a Norwegian and is sprinkled with Norwegian and Danish translations into English. Be sure to check out the links to other Viking sites, Norwegian sites, and "other barbarian pages." Lots of interesting facts about a culture from long ago.

Quest questions:

1. What does the word "Gaia" mean?

   _____

2. What were the most important export goods for the Vikings?

   _____

3. Who led the excavation of the King's Mound?

   _____

Picture this — you snap a roll of film with your 35mm camera, drop off the film to be developed, and when you arrive home your pictures are developed and waiting for you. It's now possible! Several developers allow you to drop off your 35mm or 110 film, and instead of you returning to pick up the pictures, the developer sends the pictures to your e-mail address over the Internet. You can then print the pictures on photo quality paper, create invitations or cards, or get started on a special project. It's not necessary to have a digital camera or scanner to share photographs with friends over the Internet!

Hobbies

Collect 'em All!

Website:

Kids Collecting

Address:

http://kidscollecting.miningco.com/kidsteens/kidscollecting/indexhtm?COB=looksmart

Whether you collect Beanie Babies, Barbies, stamps, shells, coins, or comics, this is the site for you. Find an extensive list of links to sites about your area of interest and meet up with other collectors in **Kids Collecting Chat**. You can sign up for a free newsletter, post questions on the site's **Bulletin Board**, and read articles about your hobby. There is information on **Safe Shopping on the Web**, something every Internet user needs to know about, and ideas for starting a new collection. Check out **In the Spotlight** for the latest articles posted on the site.

Quest questions:

1. How many links are there to other PEZ sites?

   _____

2. What information do you need to give in order to receive a free monthly newsletter?

   _____

3. How do you search for a topic on this site?

   _____

Frisbee™ Fun

Website:
Freestyle Frisbee™

Address:
http://www.frisbee.com/

Whether you are just starting out or are an advanced player wanting to learn trick throws, you can get insider tips from the pros on how to improve your Frisbee skills at this high-flying website. Review the schedule of competitions from around the world, check out **Top 25** and the **All-Time Leaders**, and explore the **Worldwide Jam Sites** around the world. Follow links to other Frisbee sites, read profiles of the world's greatest players, travel the web to the *World Flying Disc Championship*, or follow the link to *Scientific America*'s article on how a frisbee flies. There are plenty of freestyle animations to download and amazing photos to view from past world championships.

Quest questions:

1. In what direction should you shift your weight when you throw a Frisbee?

   _____

2. What is freestyle Frisbee?

   _____

3. What is a "delay" in freestyle Frisbee?

   _____

The Iditarod^{SM}

Website:

Iditarod^{SM}—The Last Great Race

Address:

http://www.iditarod.com/

Billed as "The Last Great Race on Earth," the Iditarod is a 1,150 mile dog sled race across beautiful and rugged Alaska. Find out who the mushers are, where they come from, and what motivates them to race from Anchorage to Nome in extremely harsh weather conditions such as temperatures below zero, strong winds, and treacherous hills. Start off by clicking on the **General Information** page to get background on the race. *History, Articles, and Facts* has pages filled with fascinating facts about the race. The **Teachers and Students** section has a fun *Students Playground* where you can meet Dude Dog and do simple activities. Go to the **Veterinary Corner** to find out about the dogs of the Iditarod and the care they need to survive and succeed in this tough race. Interested in becoming a musher and participating in the race? Start off by becoming a Junior Iditarod competitor—find out how by going to the **Jr. Iditarod** page. Investigate weather conditions, mileage, view maps of the race, and read diary entries from those who have made the journey. Be sure to read the incredible story of the 1925 Serum Run to Nome, which was the basis for the movie *Balto*.

Quest questions:

1. What is the Iditarod trail?

   _____

2. Who is Libby Riddles?

   _____

3. What is the Red Lantern Award?

   _____

Learn about 4-H

Website:
National 4-H Council

Address:
http://www.fourhcouncil.edu/index.htm

Learn about the opportunities available to you through the National 4-H Club and clubs in your area. Click on the **Programs** page for information about programs and initiatives going on in your area like *At the Table: Youth in Governance*, a movement to place kids on governing boards and decision making committees across the United States. At *Going Places-Making Choices*, you can help solve some of the world's environmental problems with *Energy*, *Climate*, *Land*, *People*, and *Choice*—come and share your solution suggestions and join in the discussions. Check out **Are You Into It** where you can learn about volunteerism at the grass roots level and find out how you can get involved. At **Who We Are** you can learn about the history of 4-H. Find out how you can join at **Get Involved**.

Quest questions:

1. What do the 4-H's stand for?

   _____

2. How many acres of rural land does the U.S. lose every day to development?

   _____

3. In which state was Johnny Carson involved in 4-H?

   _____

Crazy Cartoons!

Website:

Welcome to
The Cartoon Network!

Address:

http://www.cartoonnetwork.com

Doodle your way into the world of animation—Cartoon Network's animated website! Visit The Department of Cartoons' **Animation How-To** and learn how drawings are developed into full motion cartoons. Discover interesting facts about your favorite characters, or tour Hanna-Barbera Studio to learn how to cast the perfect character voice. Check out the machines used in the **Sound Room**. Sneak on over to The Scooby Doo Official Web Site and print actual pencil drawings and storyboards. Watch video clips, e-mail your favorite characters, and post your own cartoon art at this amazingly wacky website. Don't forget to speed through the *Nascar Wacky Race Game* or fly with the *Powder Puff Girls* in **Games**.

Quest questions:

1. How many episodes of the Jetsons were originally produced?

   _____

2. What breed of dog is Scooby Doo?

   _____

3. What is the essential "visual blue print of the entire cartoon?"

   _____

Perfect
Pictures

Website:

Welcome to Eastman Kodak Company℠

Address:

http://www.kodak.com/

Everything you ever wanted to know about film can be found at this comprehensive website. Go to the **Guide to Better Pictures** and learn how to take better pictures with a 35mm camera or even a disposable camera. On the **Taking Great Pictures** page the amateur photographer can learn the *Top 10 Techniques*. For the advanced photographer there are tutorials on **Basic Composition** and **Dark Room Techniques**. Click on **Doing More with your Pictures** to learn how to make unique personalized gifts from your favorite photos, like calendars and mouse pads. Learn how to get started in digital photography so that you can make picture CDs and send pictures to friends over the Internet. At **Picture This Postcard** you can send postcards to friends over the Internet using your own favorite pictures. Visit the **Digital Learning Center** and discover the new world of digital photography. Read about the technological innovations and let DLC Plus show you how ordinary people are using digital photography today.

Quest questions:

1. What is the difference between 100 speed film and 400 speed film?

   _____

2. Where does the word "photographer" come from?

   _____

3. Does a digital camera use film?

   _____

Sports
for Kids

Website:

CBS Sportsline—
Kids Zone

Address:

http://www.cbs.sportsline.com/u/kids/index.html

Choose from **Major League Baseball**, the **National Football League**, the **National Basketball Association**, or the **National Hockey League** and find out all you want to know about your favorite sport and its players. Once you enter the zone of your choice, click on **Games** to play *Defend the QB*, or maybe *Tire Toss* and then move on to the **Photos** to see snaps of the latest exciting events in sports news. Enter **Chat** to send a postcard, check out the *Birthday Tracker*, and vote in a sports poll. **Scores** lists the day's final scores, and the **Players** pages allows you to search for your favorite player either by name or by team. Listen to Roger Clemens discuss his injured hamstring and to other interviews with players in the **Audio/Video** area (you'll need Real Audio). Get team stats (colors, team manager, win/loss record) on the **Teams** page and read the latest breaking sports news when you click on **News**. A fun site for sports fans.

Quest questions:

1. Who is the team mascot for the Montreal Expos?

   _____

2. Where was John Stockton born?

   _____

3. What was Joe Gibbs' record as coach for the Washington Redskins?

   _____

You Go, Girl!

Website:

Girl Power! Campaign Homepage

Address:

http://www.health.org/gpower/

Girl Power is all about being the best, strongest, and healthiest person that you can be. Sponsored by the Department of Health and Human Services, this national public education campaign urges girls ages 8-14 to make the most of their lives and health. **BodyWise** offers information and tips on how to eat right, the importance of physical fitness, and the dangers of eating disorders. Advice from famous girl role models is sprinkled throughout the site, so check out what Brandy, Tara Lipinski, Whitney Rowe, and Picabo Street have to say in the *BodyWise Role Model* page. There are links to sports pages as well as a general list of the **Picks of the Internet**. Go to the **Games and Puzzles** page and take a nutrition quiz, solve the *Fitness Scramble* and work out the *Calcium Crossword*. The site encourages girls to contribute to the content of the site and there are several places to leave your input. Although this site is mainly for girls, boys can learn a lot about their female friends by checking it out!

Quest questions:

1. What are Whitney Rowe's hobbies?

   _____

2. What are the titles of Cassandra Walker Simmons' books?

   _____

3. Are monosaturated fats better for you than saturated fats?

   _____

Yo–Yos for Everyone!

Website:

American Yo-Yo Association:
The Official AYYA Site

Address:

http://www.pd.net/yoyo/

What toy has been around for centuries, and goes up and down in popularity? The everlasting yo-yo, of course! Log on to the American Yo-Yo Association site and get up to speed on your yo-yo facts. Read about the history of the yo-yo, and how to perform tricks from the simplest to the most advanced. There are hints on fine tuning your yo-yo as well as references to books, videos, newspapers, museums, and clubs, all dedicated to the magnificent yo-yo. Find out how Jennifer Baybrook became the World Champion Yo-Yoer and how you can compete in the world of yo-yoing. There are also pages for e-mailing other yo-yo enthusiasts (these are individuals' e-mail addresses, so be sure to follow the rules for safety on the Internet) and links to other yo-yo sites.

Quest questions:

1. Where was Richard Nixon when he yo-yoed on stage in 1974?

   _____

2. Where are the two yo-yo museums located?

   _____

3. What is the first 1999 AYYA rule?

   _____

As you tour the Internet, be sure to stop by getnetwise.com. This website was developed as a joint effort by many of the Internet powerhouses like America Online, AT&T, Bell Atlantic, MCI World Com, and Microsoft to call attention to safety concerns online. The site explores, by age, the technologies and related activities that you may explore, explains the risks, and proposes possible safeguards. The site also teaches you how to identify and report problems in cyberspace.

Museums, Tours, and Exhibits

African Heroes

Website:

AFRO-Americ@: The Black History Museum—Interactive Exhibits

Address:

http://www.afroam.org/history/history.html

This interactive website, provided by AFRO-Americ@'s Black History Museum allows you to explore America's Black heroes. Go to the **Black Resistance** page and dispel the myth that slaves were complacent and did not engage in organized resistance during the 200 year slavery period. Don't miss the moving **Tuskegee Airmen** exhibit to learn about how these brave men helped to facilitate desegregation of the United States Air Force. Check out the **Jackie Robinson** page and follow him as he becomes the first black man to play professional baseball. Discover how difficult it was for him to travel with the team when society was deeply segregated, and how some players and teams singled him out for persecution. You can also learn about the **Black Panthers, The Million Man March**, and view many advertisements from the 1920's to the 1930's for skin bleaching products in **Black or White**.

Quest questions:

1. How many slaves did Harriet Tubman help to escape from slavery?

   _____

2. What rank was Jackie Robinson in the Army?

   _____

3. The 66th Air Force Contract Flying School at the Tuskegee Institute was established for what purpose?

   _____

American Inventors

Website:

Inventure Place:
The National Inventors Hall of Fame

Address:

http://www.invent.org/inventure.html

Remember all of those inventions you made with your friends in the garage using bits of cardboard, twigs, and masking tape? Do you still have a few ideas floating around in your head? If so, this is the website for you. The **National Inventors Hall of Fame** is a tribute to the creative and innovative energy that has propelled our nation forward for the past 200 years. Look up an inventor in the alphabetical listing or by their date of induction into the Hall of Fame.

Quest questions:

1. Who was the first inventor inducted into the Hall of Fame?

   _____

2. Who was inducted into the Hall of Fame for inventing the computer mouse?

   _____

3. What was George de Mestral inducted into the hall of fame for?

   _____

Ancient Olympics

Website:

The Ancient Olympic Games
Virtual Museum

Address:

http://devlab.dartmouth.edu/olympic/

Hurl yourself back in time to Ancient Greece and wonder at the competitive splendor of the original Olympic Games. You can travel this virtual museum just like a real museum, virtually walking from room to room. In the **History** room, discover the competitive but peaceful spirit that the Greeks brought to the games and learn that the games went on even during times of war for over 1000 years. Walk through the **Anecdotes** room to learn about the truce that prevailed during the months of the Olympic Games and why court proceedings and executions were postponed during this time. Stroll through **About the Contests** to learn all about the different contests and their origins. In the *Victors Room* you can look up who won specific events for each year the Olympics were held. You can also read *Competitor Story* to get an inside glimpse of what it was like being an Olympic athlete in ancient times. In the *Panathenaia* you can visit ancient arenas and learn the rules of competition.

Quest questions:

1. In what year did the Olympics originate?

   _____

2. What did the competitors wear?

   _____

3. Were women allowed into the games?

   _____

Creating A Car

Website:

WebLINK: Auto Tour:
So You Want to Make a Car

Address:

http://www.ipl.org/autou/

This site is brought to you by the University of Michigan, where people learn about the auto industry by using computers and videoconferencing. Take a tour of the Sterling Heights Assembly Plant with Eddie Patterson, a Quality Improvement Coordinator, who is in charge of special projects. Click on **Careers with Cars** if you think you might be interested in working in the auto industry someday. Follow along the more than 16 miles of conveyors as car bodies move through the paint, and to the end of the final line by viewing photos of the process. Movies are sprinkled throughout the site and are a fun way to get a feel for the plant. At the end of the tour, you are invited to design your own company by filling out a questionnaire. See how you might succeed in the business world! Links to other automobile sites are included.

Quest questions:

1. What was the Sterling Heights Assembly Plant originally constructed for?

   _____

2. What are the three sections that an assembly plant can be divided into?

   _____

3. Why is a dashboard called a dashboard?

   _____

Discover Flight at the Air and Space Museum

Website:
The Smithsonian National Air and Space Museum

Address:
http://www.nasm.edu/

Clear the runway and get ready to take off at the Air and Space Museum's web page where you can take a virtual tour through the largest collection of historic air and spacecraft in the world. The *Milestones of Flight Exhibit* introduces the origins of modern flying and gives a glimpse of how far we have come in less than 100 years. View digital pictures of Earth from outer space and explore the unique things that make our planet able to sustain life. The **Space Race** site explores the race between the United States and Russia to be the first in space. Learn how the Russians always seemed to be one step ahead. Learn about World War aviation and the evolution of military aircraft. Discover why people can't fly without a machine at **How Things Fly**. Watch *Breaking the Sound Barrier* and discover when and how supersonic speed was reached.

Quest questions:

1. What was the first artificial satellite launched in 1957?

   _____

2. What does "supersonic" flight mean?

   _____

3. How much of the earth's surface is liquid?

   _____

Protect Your Invention

Website:
US Patent and Trademark
Office Kid's Pages

Address:
http://www.uspto.gov/go/kids/

Do you have a great idea for a product? Have you written a poem or an exciting story? All of these inventions of the mind can be protected through the US Patent and Trademark Office. You can play nine interactive games at this fantastic website, which was designed specifically for kids! Try matching inventor's names with certain clues at **Inventor IQ**, dig for historic patent information at **Trademark Treasure**, or try out the kid-friendly search engine at **We Dare You**. Design a poster, write a poem or story, or create a unique museum exhibit and enter it in the **Contests** page. Learn tips to thinking creatively at **Twinkle Lights**. There are many links to other government kid sites like the *USDA Agriculture Research*, the *IPA's Office of Wetlands*, and even the *White House!*

Quest questions:

1. What kind of property is a patent or trademark?

   _____

2. What is the most famous trade secret?

   _____

3. If you write a song and want to protect it, what should you do?

   _____

The Natural History Museum of London

Website:

The Natural History Museum

Address:

http://www.nhm.ac.uk/map/

Dive into science and take a look at the history of the natural world at this site. Start with **The Life and Earth Galleries**, where you can check out *Dinosaurs, Creepy Crawlies, Mammals and Primates*, as well as exhibits on volcanoes, earthquakes, and the development of the seas, atmosphere, and the beginnings of life. Explore the layout of the **Museum** and then head to the **Interactive** area. Delve into **QUEST** (Questioning, Understanding, Exploring Simulated Things), the **Science casebook**, and **VR fossils**. There are imaginative ideas for science projects, library and other research services, and numerous links to related sites.

Quest questions:

1. What are meteoroids?

   _____

2. What does the name "Oviraptor" mean?

   _____

3. Where is the museum's Wildlife Garden located?

   _____

The Nobel Prize

Website:

The Nobel Foundation

Address:

http://www.nobel.se/

Have you heard of someone winning the Nobel Prize? What exactly does that mean? Where does the prize come from and who decides the winners? Discover the interesting history around the prize at **The Electronic Nobel Museum Project**. Read about Alfred Nobel, a chemist, and how he provided for the Nobel Prizes in his will. Go on a virtual tour of the *Nobel Festivities* and witness the spectacular Prize Awarding Ceremony and Banquet. Sift through the *Swedish Nobel Prize Awarding Stamps* that are printed annually to commemorate the prizewinners and see what faces you recognize. Search the database of all the prizewinners and laureates—you can search by category, year, or name—and read about why they were awarded the prize.

Quest questions:

1. What was Alfred Nobel's scientific legacy?

   _____

2. Name the seven possible Nobel Prize categories.

   _____

3. For what was President Woodrow Wilson awarded the Nobel Prize for Peace in 1919?

   _____

Success

Website:
Gallery of
Achievement

Address:

http://www.achievement.org/galleryachieve.html

Ever wonder how people decide what they want to do with their lives? Ever wonder how they made it happen? Enter the **Gallery of Achievers**, part of the Academy of Achievement website, and find out how people like Francis Ford Coppola, Sir Edmund Hillary, and Oprah Winfrey made it to where they are today. Read biographies of influential individuals of the twentieth century. They are grouped by their accomplishments in: the **Arts**, **Business**, **Public Service**, **Science and Exploration**, and **Sports**. Each biography is divided into three sections—*profile, biography,* and an *interview*. Find out the characteristics that these individuals have in common by looking over **Steps to Success**. Each Step to Success is outlined and followed up with quotes from achievers. Discover how you, too, can become an achiever!

Quest questions:

1. When did Michael Eisner become CEO of the Walt Disney Company?

   _____

2. Where did Rosa Parks attend college?

   _____

3. Where does Susan Butcher live?

   _____

94

Unexplained Discoveries

Website:

The Museum of Unnatural Mystery

Address:

http://unmuseum.mus.pa.us/unmuseum.htm

Come and take a scientific look at some of the world's greatest mysteries! Is there a logical explanation for these strange happenings? Travel to the **Hall of Fame UFO Mysteries** page and discover that unidentified flying object sightings have been reported as far back as ancient times. Read about one author's theory which describes a UFO's landing and gives extraterrestrial credit for actually building the great pyramids. In the **Lost World Exhibition** you can find out about *The Ape Man of the Mountains*, *Big Foot*, and how people have spotted mammoth human-like creatures in mountain ranges around the world. Check out **Odd Archeology** and read about the *Lost City of Atlantis* and the *Curse of the Mummy*. Visit the **Virtual Exploration Society** and discover amazing tales of explorers as they travel into harm's way in search of adventure. They descend into the *Amazon*, mingle with the *Mountain Gorillas of Africa*, open the *Tomb of King Tut*, and race to the *North Pole*. In the **Mad Scientists Laboratory** you can create your own adventures like building a balloon rocket or growing your own crystals.

Quest questions:

1. What is the largest known snake in the world?

   _____

2. What is the penalty for killing "Big Foot" in Skamania County, Washington?

   _____

3. What is the largest and oldest pyramid?

   _____

Wow! What a Museum!

Website:

The Exploratorium:
The Museum of Science, Art,
and Human Perception

Address:

http://www.exploratorium.edu/

Visit the online version of this superb San Francisco museum. There are 650 science, art, and human perception exhibits that rotate through the **Exploratorium** and you can visit them all online. Check out the current exhibits as well as looking up past exhibits in the online digital library. There is information on the museum's background, including the history of the **Palace of Fine Arts** where the Exploratorium is housed. The site is updated daily, so return again and again and enjoy the Exploratorium from wherever in the world you might be. Seven million people visit this museum's site each year—find out why!

Quest questions:

1. When was the Exploratorium founded?

   _____

2. Who was the designer of the Palace of Fine Arts?

   _____

3. What is the street address of the Exploratorium?

   _____

While your computer keyboard doesn't allow you to reproduce natural elements of real-time communication like body language and voice inflections, it *does* allow you some alternatives.

Try these!

Happy	:-)	Wink	;-)
Sad	:'-(	See nothing x-)
Surprise	:-o	Say nothing :-x

Nature

A Whale of a Time!

Website:

WhaleTimes Seabed

Address:

http://www.whaletimes.org/

Sea animals are the name of the game at this site! Go to the **Fishin' for Facts** page and learn all about killer whales, elephant seals, giant squid, and more. If you have a question about one of the animals, or a sea animal that is not listed, go to **Ask Jake, the Seadog** and see if your question is posted there. If not, send your question to Jake and he will try to respond to you within seven days. Try to identify parts of a whale at *Whale Puzzler*, and then read *Whale Tale*, a neverending story, and add your own twist to the tale. **Sea of Books** lists favorite references on sea animals as well as an extensive bibliography. **Leviathan Links** has many great marine science sites that you may want to explore when you are finished at **WhaleTimes**.

Quest questions:

1. How big was the largest recorded giant squid?

   _____

2. What is the mission of WhaleTimes?

   _____

3. What does a whale use its pectoral flippers for?

   _____

Animals, Animals: The Electronic Zoo

Website:
The Electronic Zoo

Address:
http://netvet.wustl.edu/e-zoo.htm

Designed and continually updated by veterinarian Ken Boschert, this site has information about many different animals, as well as on the field of veterinary medicine. Dr. Boschert has done a great job combining his knowledge of animals with his knowledge of the Internet. If you can't find what you are looking for on his site, he has set up links to many other search engines as well. Be sure to check out the **Pick of the Litter**, a weekly animal related website, and read the interesting history of how his site came to be. This is a huge site, with easy access to all kinds of animal related information.

Quest questions:

1. What is "A Breed Apart"?

   _____

2. What does ASPCA stand for?

   _____

3. Where is the Ross University School of Veterinary Medicine?

   _____

Explore National Parks

Website:

ParkNet: Gateway to the
National Park Service

Address:

http://www.nps.gov/index.html

Come and discover the rich and varied landscape of America at the **National Park Service** website. The site provides extensive history and information about public parks in the United States. Be sure to check out **Links to the Past** to find out about historic happenings in our National Park System. You can look up parks by name, state, theme, or historical significance to view a park map and find out specific visiting information. You can even make camping reservations for your summer trip! Visit **Nature Net** to discover the biodiversity in the park system from air and water quality to the geological makeup of a park. Learn all about the public and private organizations that help the park system to be successful at **Park Smart**. At the **Info Zone** you can learn about what goes into park planning and catch up on current legislation affecting the park system.

Quest questions:

1. What country gave the Statue of Liberty to the United States over 100 years ago?

   _____

2. How long is the Grand Canyon in miles?

   _____

3. What is the most visited park in the National Park System with over 9 million visitors a year?

   _____

Green Thumb's Garden

Website:

Garden.com—
Gardening for Today's World

Address:

http://www.garden.com/

Grab a pair of gloves and get ready to dig your way into beautiful plants and flowers for the garden. For those of you who have never grown anything except mold, this is a great site for learning about our oxygen-producing friends. Look up a plant, find out if it is an annual or perennial, and see if it can grow in your specific climate zone. Go to **Kid's Gardening Camp** for tips on gardening for kids of any age! Find references to books that will help you create gardens that can attract certain birds and butterflies. Discover what you are supposed to do in your garden in certain months or ask a plant question at the **Garden Doctor**. Whether your thumb is green or not, there is sure to be something useful and interesting for you at this site.

Quest questions:

1. What is the difference between an annual and a perennial?

   _____

2. What is the State Tree of Alaska? (What is your State Tree?)

   _____

3. What is the name for plant science?

   _____

Know Your Pets

Website:

PetStation Kids!

Address:

http://petstation.com/kids.html

Do you have a pet and want to learn more about it? Are you thinking about adopting a pet, but are not sure what type of pet is best for you? **Pet Station** offers all sorts of information in the *Bird Barn*, *Cat Cabana*, *Dog Domain*, *Fish Fair*, *Herp Hacienda*, *Horse Heaven*, and the *Small Mammal Medley*. Hop aboard the **E-Train** to visit the Bird Barn. Check out the **Library** to look up information on different species, read interesting articles, and find links to bird clubs and publications. Stop in **Bird Banter** to chat with people about your feathered friends or seek advice from other bird owners. You can travel to each of the animal areas to explore libraries, chat rooms, photo galleries of the different animals, or to check out the pets for sale.

Quest questions:

1. What is the one animal besides humans that is capable of human speech?

   _____

2. What is a "herp"?

   _____

3. Can you use ordinary table salt to add salinity to a saltwater tank?

   _____

The National Severe Storms Laboratory

Website:
NSSL Educational Information

Address:
http://www.nssl.noaa.gov/edu/

This is a well done introductory site to basic weather. Find out the **What, Where, Whys, and Hows** on *tornadoes*, *hurricanes*, *lightning*, and *thunderstorms*. Wonderful photographs accompany the different topics, each of which is broken down into a question and answer format, i.e. where do hurricanes come from and what kind of damage can they do? Move on to **Weather Lessons** and see what kind of weather symbols are used, and then make up some of your own. Scan weather maps and discover why weather systems exist. Want to chase tornadoes for a living? Learn how to prepare yourself for a career in weather when you go to the **Weather Careers** page. Check out other great weather links listed under **Interesting Weather Sites**. You can also e-mail questions to the website masters at the National Severe Storms Laboratory.

Quest questions:

1. What are cloud flashes?

   _____

2. When was the first weather map developed?

   _____

3. What are the three main areas for meteorologists?

   _____

Outrageous Earthquakes

Website:

Earthquake Information
from the USGS

Address:

http://quake.wr.usgs.gov/

Come and see what's shaking at this earthquake site. Visit **Latest Quake Information** and check out up to the minute details about earthquake activity in areas around the world. Did you know that earthquakes may be taking place under your feet right now, but may be too small to feel? Go to **What's New or Interesting** to learn if earthquake prediction is possible and how soil type effects an earthquake. At **Hazards and Preparedness** you can find out how to prepare yourself for an earthquake and identify the many hazards that can occur. Discover how scientists study earthquakes and learn all about faults and why they cause earthquakes at the **Studying Earthquakes** page. Check out your geographical area on the map and see if there has been any recent shift in the earth.

Quest questions:

1. What should you do immediately if you find yourself in an earthquake?

   _____

2. Can a certain weather pattern cause an earthquake?

   _____

3. How many earthquakes does the National Earthquake Information Center report every year?

   _____

Sunny or Rainy?

Website:

Rain or Shine Weather

Address:

http://www.rainorshine.com

At this site, you can enter your city, or any city in the United States or around the world, and get a complete five-day forecast of the weather. Click on one of the three maps and get a visual 24-hour forecast, a satellite reading, or a Nexrad Radar demonstration. Another fun feature is the **Old Farmer's Almanac** at the bottom of the page. Go to *History* to see what happened on any day in the past. In *Weather History*, you can get some free friendly advice, and try to answer the question of the day. You can also browse through the Almanac's archives in **Ask the Almanac**. Want to know when the next solar or lunar eclipse will be? Go to **Heavenly Details**, where you can also find the dates on which a full moon will occur for the next five years.

Quest questions:

1. On what day in September 2000 is a full moon expected?

   _____

2. Who produces the website **Rain or Shine Weather**?

   _____

3. What is the weather forecast for Hilton Head Island today?

   _____

Swimming with Sea Turtles

Website:

Turtle Trax-A Sea Turtle Page

Address:

http://www.turtles.org/

Meet Clothahump, the sea turtle that inspired this web page, and read about her last sighting in 1993 at the **Dedication Page**. Learn about fibropapilloma tumors and how they are a threat to all sea turtles. Read **All About Sea Turtles** and discover the many types of sea turtles, their similarities and differences, and learn why most species of sea turtles are endangered around the world. In the **Kidz Corner** there are many great stories to read about the triumphs and tragedies of the marine turtles, activities to print, and even directions for making a turtle sundae. Check out **Turtle Happenings** to catch up on current turtle news from around the world. Visit **How You Can Help** to learn the many ways that you can help the marine turtles.

Quest questions:

1. What do green sea turtles primarily eat?

   _____

2. Why do groups of fish follow these turtles?

   _____

3. How much does the largest leather-back turtle on record weigh?

   _____

Trek the Zoo

Website:

World Famous San Diego Zoo

Address:

http://www.sandiegozoo.org/

Go on a cyber safari into the Ituri Forest and explore the depths of the African Forest. Meet the Mbuti people and view their leaf-shingled huts, travel on to the **River's Edge** to mingle with the hippopotamus, then walk through the **Bamboo Corridor** to see the beautiful and colorful birds of the African forest. Watch out for the forest buffalo herd! This virtual tour is developing further and promises new surprises every time you return. At **Star Treks** you are introduced to a San Diego Zoo celebrity animal every week. Learn about its size, food sources, habitat, and social structure, and search for animals that have been featured in the past. At **Animals at Large** you can research all types of animals at the zoo from the most peculiar reptile to the most docile mammals. Stroll through **Plant Place** to learn about the zoo's equally interesting botanical gardens. In the **Learning Section** you can send postcards or play games like *Try Naming the Baby Names* for all of the animals.

Quest questions:

1. What does the word "hippopotamus" mean?

   _____

2. How much water can a camel drink at one time?

   _____

3. What do the Mbuti people make their huts out of?

   _____

It's good for your mind to read and learn, but it's good for your soul to sit and chat. In this Internet age, it is now possible to converse through e-mail in real time. One friend logged onto the Internet can instantaneously exchange messages with another friend logged onto the Internet thousands of miles away! This growing feature is sometimes referred to as instant messaging. Several Internet Service Providers (ISPs) offer their own brand of this technology and usually you can only exchange instant messages within an ISP. If someone you don't know sends you an instant message, close the window and don't respond.

Reading and Learning

All About Words

Website:

WordCentral.Com—Home Page

Address:

http://www.wordcentral.com/home.html

Word Central can not only help with homework problems, but it is fun as well. Start off by looking up words in the **Student Dictionary**, where you will find pronunciation, function, and definition. Enter the hallway and take a tour of the first floor. Start off in the cafeteria and check out the **Buzzword of the Day**, where you will learn a new word, it's meaning, how you use it, and other related words. There is also a **Daily Buzzword Archive**, and a place to subscribe to the *Daily Buzzword*. (It's free when you supply your first name and e-mail address.) Compose your own original rhyming poem in the **Music Room**, enter new words in the **Build Your Own Dictionary Room**, and send a message in Morse Code and other languages in the **Science Lab**. You can also send an encoded message to a friend from the **Computer Lab**. See what fun words can be!

Quest questions:

1. When was the first Merriam-Webster Dictionary issued? (Hint: Go to the **Teachers' Lounge**.)

   _____

2. What does "placid" mean and what is its function?

   _____

3. What are three words that rhyme with absurd? (Hint: Go to the **Music Room**.)

   _____

Animals, Myths, and Legends

Website:

Animals, Myths, and Legends:
Tales from Oban
the Knowledge Keeper

Address:

http://www.ozemail.com.au/~oban/

Meet Oban the Knowledge Keeper, Agor the Chinese Dragon, and Sanjit, Oban's great nephew, at this fun-filled site. Go to the **Legends** page and read *How the Bear Lost his Tail*, *Coyote Brings Fire*, and *The Ungrateful Tiger*. There is a long list of legends to choose from, each of which tells a great story with a good moral. The **Playroom** has a coloring book to print out, crossword puzzles to solve, and many very good word searches on topics like U.S. lakes, pizza words, and sci-fi. Follow links to other good play sites within the **Playroom** page. The **Animals** page has facts about different animals as well as photographs.

Quest questions:

1. Where did the *Rabbit the Hunter* legend come from?

   _____

2. What is the first word in the *Bake a Cake* word search?

   _____

3. How tall is Wally the Wombat?

   _____

Beverly Cleary

Website:

The Unofficial
Beverly Cleary Home Page

Address:

http://www.teleport.com/~krp/cleary.html

Meet Ramona the Pest, Henry Huggins, Beezus, Ribsy and the rest of the gang! Beverly Cleary, the renowned author of books for children, has been writing her wonderful books for almost fifty years. Find out how she got started and how she comes up with all of her crazy characters. You can read her biography, get a comprehensive list of the books that she has written, and read comments from some of her many fans. The site highlights a different book each month and posts reviews and excerpts from the book. Go to **Frequently Asked Questions** and find out how to get in touch with Ms. Cleary. Be sure to sign the **Guestbook** and let everyone know what your favorite Beverly Cleary book is.

Quest questions:

1. When did Beverly Cleary publish *Henry Huggins*?

   _____

2. What is the last book in the Klickitat Street series?

   _____

3. Where did Beverly Cleary meet her husband?

   _____

Games Galore

Website:

FunBrain.com

Address:

http://www.funbrain.com/

FunBrain is home to over thirty online games, divided into eight subjects. Choose a subject or click on your age group to see a list of games. Games for ages 7 through 10 include *Stay Afloat*, which is similar to Hangman, *Math Baseball*, a numbers game, and *Spellaroo*, where you can test your spelling ability. These are just a few of the twenty games available within the 7 to 10 age group. If you register with the site, a record will be kept of the games you have played and what your scores were, but registering is optional. Check out the character biographies for a good laugh. There are also pages for teachers and parents, as well as games for ages 15 and up. Watch out—you may end up fighting over who's going to get to play next!

Quest questions:

1. What are the names of Priscilla Gorilla's children?

   _____

2. What is the object of the *Change Maker* game?

   _____

3. When was John Adams President of the United States?

   _____

Get to Know Your World

Website:

ePlay—A Site for Play and Learning

Address:

http://eplay.com/home.adp

Join Sasha, Malcolm, Tatsuo, and Ali as they team up against the evil villain, Dr. XED. These four bugs will take you on exciting adventures through Greece, England, Peru, the United States, and Egypt, where you can have fun and learn about other countries and cultures at the same time. Go to **Explore Your World**, choose a country, and click on *Famous Faces*, *Famous Places*, *Wild Things*, or *Stuff to Do*. The photographs and activities are great. Be sure to check out **Bug Libs**, where you make up a story by filling in specific kinds of words, i.e. a noun, an action verb, or an adjective. The story you end up with can be hilarious! Join the *eBUGS Club* (it's free!) and the site will keep track of all your game scores, let you exchange e-mail with other club members, and send club news via e-mail.

Quest questions:

1. What is "Nile slime"?

   _____

2. What time did Maria Reiche get up in the morning?

   _____

3. Which two seas lie between the United Kingdom and Norway?

   _____

Homework Resources

Website:

B.J. Pinchbeck's Homework Helper

Address:

http://www.bjpinchbeck.com

B.J. Pinchbeck is a twelve-year-old student who started this website in 1996 with the assistance of his dad. It has grown quickly and has won over 100 awards on the Internet. Start out by finding out a little bit about "Beege" by going to **Frequently Asked Questions**. Let the research begin! There are pages for **Search Engines** (a nice reference to have), reference sites such as dictionaries, encyclopedias and thesauruses, and a page for **News and Current Events** sites. These pages are followed by listings of sites for school subjects like math, social studies, and history. After all that learning, go to the **Playtime** page and find some fun sites to explore. Beege has also put together a spelling list, search tips, and a collection of family photos. A great reference site—and a kid did it!

Quest questions:

1. What is B.J.'s favorite search engine?

   _____

2. What is the other name for Bonus.com?

   _____

3. Is B.J. Pinchbeck homeschooled?

   _____

Kids' Books

Website:

Bookworm: Great Books
for Kids 6-12

Address:

http://www.kidsreads.com

Do you stay up late reading books with a flashlight in bed? Do you ever wonder how someone comes up with the ideas for books or a book series? Are you tired of the same old stories and want to find something new to read? If so, this website is for you. There are book reviews galore written by kids for kids. Search for a book by topic, reading level, or by the author's name. Sign up on the **Wish List** page and then bookmark the titles that you are interested in. Parents and friends have access to the list so they will know what kind of books you like to read. Join the **Book Club** and win prizes for reading or send in your own book reviews. Read the **Bookworm Newsletter** to find new leads to great books. You can even read and print out books online at the **Bookworm Bookshelf**. Check out **Meet the Authors** and get to know some of your all-time favorites. Learn the secrets behind some of their characters and how they feel about important literary issues like censorship.

Quest questions:

1. Who was Judy Blume's character Fudge named after?

   _____

2. When Laura Ingalls Wilder's husband died in 1942, how long had they been married?

   _____

3. What author won the 1963 Presidential Medal of Freedom and 1971 National Medal for Literature and received seven honorary degrees from colleges and universities for his literary contributions?

   _____

Pirates, Tropical Islands, and Treasure

Website:

Treasure Island

Address:

http://www.ukoln.ac.uk/services/treasure/contents.htm

Meet Robert Louis Stevenson and get the inside scoop on *Treasure Island*, the story he wrote for his stepson in 1881. Get to know Jim Hawkins, Billy Bones, and Long John Silver when you go to the **Characters** page and find out the basics of the story when you read the **Plot**. You can even read the entire story online, chapter by chapter. Click on the links and explore ships, pirates, tropical islands, and treasure sites. After you have read the story, go to the **Things to Do** page and try your hand at the *Treasure Island Quiz*, *Design a Pirate*, or *Captain Dave's Treasure Hunt*. There are references to other pirate stories under **Library Stuff**, as well as spots to e-mail the website and do a book review of *Treasure Island*. When you are all done, go to the library and check out a copy of the book!

Quest questions:

1. What happens to Long John Silver at the end of the book?

   _____

2. What occupation does Ben Gunn take up when he returns to England?

   _____

3. Where does the story begin?

   _____

The computer, like your brain, stores and processes vast amounts of information and performs many tasks at one time. Your computer's brain is a silicon chip. This tiny silicon wafer enables the computer to perform millions of calculations per second. New technological discoveries make it possible for chip manufacturers to produce chips that are smaller and more powerful. As this happens, the opportunities for computerizing objects other than the classic computer become greater. In the not-too-distant future, there will be smart appliances like cell phones that can forecast the weather or cars that can direct themselves to your destination.

Science

Do You See What I See?

Website:

Sandlot Science.com:
Optical Illusions

Address:

http://www.lainet.com/~ausbourn/

Is that a young girl or an old woman? Wait...it's both! Discover the many varieties of optical illusions on this creative and fun website. Choose from **Impossible Objects**, **Ambiguous Figures**, **Typography**, and more. Read about the **Giants of Illusion** and find out who is behind these mind tricks. Be sure to check out the **Games and Puzzles** page, particularly the *Mysterious Mind Reader* and *Ohio Blue Tips*. The site is full of live demonstrations, artwork, animation, stories, projects, games, and puzzles. It appears to be updated monthly, so check back to see what has been added since your last visit.

Quest questions:

1. Who is Jerry Andrus?

   _____

2. What are Ohio blue tips?

   _____

3. What is a moire pattern?

   _____

Experience Energy

Website:

Energy Quest

Address:

http://www.energy.ca.gov/education/

It is dark, so you turn on the light. It is cold, so you turn on the heat. Your clothes are dirty, so you throw them in the wash. What do light, heat, and the washing machine have in common? Electricity is a form of energy that we don't think much about until it fails us. The **Energy Quest** website explores all types of energy from electricity to nuclear power. Power up at the **Energy Story** where you find friendly explanations about electricity, generators, turbines, nuclear energy, solar energy, and much more. Visit **Fossil Fuels** and learn why it is important not to waste these precious resources. Visit the **Alternative Fuel Vehicles** page to learn about alternatives to gasoline and why we must develop new types of fuel. Test your knowledge of energy at **Watt's That**, the Internet's only energy game show. Brush up on the recent developments in energy in **Poor Richard's Energy Almanac.** (Energy as we know it is a fairly recent development!) Don't forget to visit **Science Projects** and get ready to impress friends at your next science fair.

Quest questions:

1. What are the three major forms of fossil fuels?

   _____

2. What does hydroelectric mean?

   _____

3. What substance fuels nuclear plants?

   _____

Genetic Secrets

Website:

Innovation—
Cracking the Code

Address:

http://www.wnet.org/archive/innovation/

Explore the fascinating world of genetics and learn about how your genetic makeup effects you in every aspect of your life. This website, which is based on a PBS series with the same name, is divided into three programs. In **Program One: Cracking the Code** you can learn how genetic engineering helps fight disease, but that some people feel genetic engineering may result in harmful consequences. Discover what genes are, and how they mutate. In **Program Two: The Man-Made Man**, learn about how modern science has lengthened man's life span and learn about the new trails being blazed in biotechnology. In **Program Three: Live Long and Prosper**, discover the many new treatments that are saving the lives of stroke victims and helping Parkinson's patients fight the effects of this debilitating disease. You will leave this website with a genuine respect for modern science and medicine.

Quest questions:

1. Is it possible for one person to carry a gene for a deadly disease and never know it?

   _____

2. Where is a cell's genetic information stored?

   _____

3. During a stroke, blood flow to what vital organ is interrupted?

   _____

122

Infectious Diseases

Website:

American Museum
of Natural History:
Infection Detection Protection

Address:

http://www.amnh.org/explore/infection/index.html

Come and meet the oldest form of life on earth, the microbe. You can't see them with the naked eye, but they can be found everywhere, especially at this website dedicated to bacteria. Go to the **Infection** page and learn the many ways infections can enter your body. If harmful bacteria are everywhere, why don't we get sick all of the time? Play the **Amazing Microbe Hunters** and discover the personalities behind major discoveries in bacteria. Play the Shockwave version of **Infection**, where you are the germ and try to break down a human's defense system. Choose to be different bacteria like influenza, rabies, or tetanus. Check out **How Lou Got the Flu** and learn how she caught a virus from a duck in China and how that virus traveled clear across the world to make her sick. Visit the **Prevention Convention** to learn tips to avoid infection, like not eating raw cookie dough.

Quest questions:

1. What did Edward Jenner discover in 1796?

   _____

2. What did Alexander Fleming discover growing on bread that lead to the discovery of penicillin and other antibiotics?

   _____

3. What is your bodies second line of defense against germs?

   _____

The Periodic Table

Website:

A Visual Interpretation
of the Table of Elements

Address:

http://www.chemsoc.org/viselements/

Everything in the universe is made up of some combination of 109 elements on the periodic table. Each of these elements can be explored in depth at this website. Come and learn how the organization of the elements developed into the periodic table and how the scientist who discovered it, born to a poor family in Western Siberia, lived before the discovery of atomic number and energy level. View the amazing computer generated pictures at **Periodic Landscapes** and then send an e-mail postcard to a friend. You can even download screen savers of titanium and desktop patterns of hydrogen or lithium.

Quest questions:

1. How many known elements make up the periodic table?

   _____

2. Who is credited with the discovery of the periodic table?

   _____

3. What colorless and odorless gas makes up 21% of the Earth's atmosphere?

   _____

Relics from the Past

Website:

Thornton's Natural Discovery—
Dinosaurs, Fossils, and Gems

Address:

http://www.discovery.thorntons.co.uk/

This is a good example of a modest site. Sponsored by Thornton's Chocolate Factory in the United Kingdom, the site's purpose is to help people look toward the future by understanding the past. There are six areas to explore: **Gemstones**, **Dinosaurs**, **Fossils**, **Nature**, **News**, and of course, **Chocolate**— all contain interesting and useful information. Start out at the cave and click on one of the six areas. You can check out your birthstone at the **Gemstones** page, learn how fossils form at the **Fossils** page, and trace the evolution of dinosaurs at the **Dinosaur** page. Don't forget the **Chocolate** page, where you can discover how chocolate came to be! Thank goodness!

Quest questions:

1. When did dinosaurs appear on the earth?

   _____

2. Where do most of the world's cacao beans come from?

   _____

3. Where are sapphires formed?

   _____

Satellites in Space

Website:

Tech Museum:
The Satellite Site

Address:

http://www.thetech.org/hyper/satellite/

Blast off into outer space with the Satellite site and learn about satellites and how they work. Satellites perform all sorts of tasks, like communication, charting weather patterns, and intelligence mapping for the military. Discover why satellites travel different orbits based upon their task, speed, and distance from the earth. Click on **Space Junk** to learn about all sorts of things floating around the Earth's atmosphere—most of which we put there. Visit the **Satellite Site of the Month** to learn about new satellites being built and advances in satellite technology. Try constructing your own satellite with the online **Satellite Construction Set**. Investigate all of the smaller systems that work together to make up a large complex satellite. It is out of this world!

Quest questions:

1. How long does it take a satellite in Low Earth Orbit to circle the entire planet?

   _____

2. What powers most of the satellites?

   _____

3. What is the difference between a Low Earth Orbit and a Polar Orbit?

   _____

Science is Fun

Website:

The Learning Web at the
U.S. Geological Survey

Address:

http://www.usgs.gov/education/

Learn about how plants, animals, land, water, and maps are part of biology, geology, hydrology, and geography, and how these sciences help us to understand our world. **Land and People: Finding a Balance** shows how people and the environment interact and change the ecosystem. See the changes that have come about in Cape Cod, Los Angeles, and the Everglades. The first page has photographs and short paragraphs about each of the three regions. To find out more, go to the *Student Guide* at the end of each region's description. **Adventures in the Learning Web** lists sites on acid rain, Mt. St. Helens, the Ocoee River, marine biology, and many other topics. Click on **Adventure Continues Beyond the USGS** for science sites outside the USGS. **Living in the Learning Web** addresses topics like earthquakes, radon gas, and the source of household water. **Teaching in the Learning Web** is a wonderful lesson plan and activity resource for parents and teachers. The material is presented in a straightforward way and the site is easy to navigate.

Quest questions:

1. What is a bog?

_____

2. Where is the Cherokee National Forest located?

_____

3. What is the average rain pH in Washington, D.C.?

_____

Science with Beakman and Jax

Website:

You Can with Beakman and Jax

Address:

http://www.beakman.com/

Come and find the answers to all sorts of off the wall questions at this wacky website based upon the popular television show. Experiment with the **Interactive Demos**—check out what makes a remote control work or find out what earwax is made of. Click on **Answers to Your Questions** and discover *You Can 50*, which contains answers to the most commonly asked questions, like "How do you make Silly Putty" or "Why do I hear weird sounds at night?" Perhaps you can try a few of the easy experiments and activities at home. View pictures from the Hubble Telescope and you may actually see a star being born! Nose around the **Beakman's World Tour** to find out if the television show will be travelling to your area.

Quest questions:

1. What is a diamond made out of?

   _____

2. Do things get bigger or smaller when they warm up?

   _____

3. During thunder there is a thrust of sound waves from an electric explosion. What is it called?

   _____

Space Out!

Website:

Students for the
Exploration and Development
of Space (SEDS)

Address:

http://www.seds.org/

This website is hosted by the University of Arizona chapter of Students for the Exploration and Development of Space. The site is broken down into topics such as **Space, Astronomy, and Rocketry**. Go to **Tour the Galaxy** for basic information on *Planets, Astronomy, Aerospace,* and *Visions.* You can go to the **Mars Exploration** page and view images of Mars taken from the Hubble Space Telescope and get facts and information about the planet. Want to watch the next space shuttle? The launch schedule can be found on the **Space** page. Check out **SETI: The Search for Extra Terrestrial Intelligence** and decide for yourself whether life exists on other planets. You can also search for space-related topics and get answers from the SEDS experts by sending them e-mail. A great site to inspire students interested in the wonders of space exploration and travel.

Quest questions:

1. Where was SEDS founded?

   _____

2. How many constellations are there?

   _____

3. What is the diameter of Saturn?

   _____

Why Garbage Stinks

Website:

The Rotten Truth
About Garbage

Address:

http://www.astc.org/info/exhibits/rotten/rthome.htm

Phew! This site really stinks! Visit **What is Garbage** to find out exactly what it is that we throw away. Then go to **There's No "Away"** to learn that no matter what we do to our garbage, there is some of it that we can't get rid of. Check out the *Garbage timeline* to see how Americans have disposed of their garbage over the years—like how they buried armor in holes during the 1700's or how New York stopped dumping its garbage from a platform into the East River in the mid 1800's. From there check out **Nature Recycles** and discover the natural process of decomposition and how some types of garbage are good for us. At the **Making Choices** page you learn all sorts of ways to reduce your families garbage, from choosing products with less packaging waste or products that are partially recycled. At the **Activity Center** you can take a tour of a landfill and enjoy an interactive exhibit on how it works, or find directions for constructing a compost heap or a soda bottle bioreactor. Take the **Trash Audit** to find out how much waste is generated in your home or school.

Quest questions:

1. How much garbage does America generate every year?

   _____

2. What living thing is a natural decomposer?

   _____

3. How long does it take newspaper to decompose? A soda can?

   _____

Answer Key

Page 12 .... **Link with Kids around the World**

1. 1990
2. Norway
3. Europe, Africa, Asia, Pacific, North America, Central and South America

Page 13 .... **Surf Monkey™: An Internet Guide**

1. Reviews, Tips, Multiplayer, PC, Video Console Games, and Web-Based Games
2. Check the criteria and then send e-mail to the site's address.
3. The Louvre

Page 14 .... **What Does That Mean?**

1. Transmission Control Protocol/Internet Protocol
2. Aim and Plan
3. At IBM's research laboratory in Zurich, Switzerland

Page 16 .... **Art Adventures**

1. She was a maid.
2. Vincent Van Gogh
3. Over 20,000

Page 17 .... **The Art of Origami**

1. Senbazuru Orikata : How to Fold One Thousand Cranes
2. 100 AD in China (They managed to keep it a secret from the world for 500 years!)
3. Kikaizuki Washi

Page 18 .... **Fun on the Internet**

1. Devin, Jessie, and Zach
2. Build your own town
3. Paint! Draw! Share! Surf!

Page 19 .... **The Grammy™ Awards**

1. A National Academy member or a record company
2. 1990
3. An independent accounting firm

Page 20 .... **The Noise of Music**

1. Strings, Brass, Woodwinds, and Percussion
2. The number of times per second that something vibrates
3. The flute

Page 21 .... Paul Cézanne

1. January 19, 1839
2. National Gallery of Art, Washington, D.C.
3. 70 x 82 cm

Page 24 .... Arnold Schwarzenegger

1. John Kimble
2. 20 years old
3. Katherine, Christina, Patrick, and Christopher

Page 25 .... Dirty Harry: Hero of the Screen

1. Italy
2. 1986-88
3. Rawhide

Page 26 .... Fun on the Web

1. Write to him at Squigly@SquiglysPlayhouse.com
2. Yes!
3. Yes!

Page 27 .... Games and Fun

1. Send an e-mail with your request.
2. Kids!
3. No

Page 28 .... Hollywood People

1. 1989
2. February 21, 1979
3. Lay it Down

Page 29 .... The Making of A Documentary

1. A crash box is the box used to house the camera so it will not be destroyed by the avalanche.
2. "Fire in the Hole" is what people yell when they drop explosives into a hole in order to trigger an avalanche.
3. The producer of the film

Page 30 .... MTV™ Backstage

1. Water Skiing
2. Ringo Starr
3. (Answers will vary.)

Page 31 .... Nintendo™ Rules!

1. Kyoto, Japan
2. Japanese playing cards
3. 9

Page 32 .... The Oscars℠

1. Academy Award of Merit
2. Gold-plated britannium
3. A knight with a sword standing on a reel of film

Page 33 .... Ride a Roller Coaster

1. Super Man the Escape at Six Flags Magic Mountain, Valencia, CA
2. 7,400 feet
3. 1927

Page 36 .... Cooking for Kids

1. To remove from the freezer until soft
2. Refrigeration
3. A tool used for stirring

Page 37 .... Ice Cream for the People

1. Oberlin College in Ohio
2. 537 Saint Ann Street, Jackson Square, New Orleans, LA 70116
3. $8.00

Page 38 .... Jelly Beans!

1. 1965
2. Monday-Sunday from 9 am-5pm (closed some holidays)
3. Only four calories per bean!

Page 39 .... Yummy Candy

1. 50 or more!
2. Denmark
3. Yes

Internet Quest

Page 42 .... Answers for Just About Everything

1. Counter-clockwise
2. 57,000
3. 550 liters or 150 cubic feet

Page 43 .... For Your Health

1. Artery
2. Oxygen
3. Sound

Page 44 .... Questions, Questions

1. Calcium
2. Chester Arthur
3. Nile, Amazon, and Yangtze

Page 45 .... Stocks, Bonds, and Investing

1. Money you pay the government from the money you earn
2. You are part owner of that company.
3. Bull market: a market that steadily rises over time
   Bear market: a market that declines over time

Page 46 .... Tobacco Road

1. It narrows your blood vessels and puts added strain on your heart
2. Nearly four million, according to data released in 1997
3. Most people start before they finish high school!

Page 47 .... World News for Kids

1. James Naismith
2. Increased
3. Communism

Page 48 .... Where Are They Now?

1. Ms. Lyon was the founder of Mount Holyoke College.
   She is buried in South Hadley, Massachusetts.
2. He was killed by a pitched ball while playing for the Dayton, Ohio ballclub in 1909.
3. The musician who wrote "Jingle Bells"

Page 49 .... Yahooligans™

1. File Transfer Protocol—an application used to download things from the Internet
2. Catherine
3. Blue Streak, Tidal Wave, Top Gun, Demon, Grizzly, or Vortex

Page 52 .... America the Great

1. China and India
2. Delaware
3. Rhode Island

Page 53 .... Explore Antarctica

1. No
2. Less than an inch
3. 98%

Page 54 .... Investigate the Loch Ness Monster

1. 40 meters
2. The Vikings
3. Throwing a tall tree trunk — some are almost 20 feet tall!

Page 55 .... Learn a Language

1. "Non capisco."
2. "Je le prends."
3. "¿Dónde está el baño?"

Page 56 .... Map the World

1. 2821.1
2. Denver to Chicago
3. (Answers will vary.)

Page 57 .... The Peace Corps

1. John F. Kennedy
2. 18 years old
3. 1974

Page 58 .... Pharaohs and Pyramids

1. Mrs. Suzanne Mubarak
2. 40
3. 1798

Page 59 .... Safe Spelunking

1. Ruby Falls in Chattanooga, TN
2. Icicles
3. Mammoth Cave in Kentucky

Page 60 .... **Sky Scrapers**

1. The Petronas Tower #1 and #2 in Kuala Lampur
2. Frank Lloyd Wright
3. The Sears Tower

Page 61 .... **South Dakota: A Guide to the Great Sioux Nation**

1. 1803
2. 244,000 acres
3. Dakota

Page 62 .... **Tower of London**

1. Boys and girls
2. Raw eggs
3. Mary

Page 63 .... **The World's Most Incredible Places**

1. The yak
2. Argentina
3. Papyrus

Page 66 .... **All About Money**

1. 100,000
2. 52.5 million
3. The eye symbolizes divine guidance.

Page 67 .... **The British Monarchy**

1. Edward III
2. George II in 1743
3. The Union Jack

Page 68 .... **Early American Pioneers**

1. To settle on public land to use as a home
2. The captain, or wagon master
3. The author of *Rebecca of Blossom Prairie*

Page 69 .... **Famous Explorers**

1. $100 a year
2. Three
3. The Spirit of St. Louis

Page 70 .... **Fly with the Blue Angels**

1. 3,000
2. The plane that transports the Blue Angels stuff
3. 140,000

Page 71 .... **The Lewis and Clark Expedition**

1. The Corp of Discovery
2. Sixteen
3. To find a water route to the Pacific Ocean

Page 72 .... **Meet Anne Frank**

1. Over two years
2. Miep Gies and Bep Voskuijl
3. One. The survivor was Anne's father, Otto Frank.

Page 73 .... **The Titanic in Cyber Space**

1. 2,223
2. First Officer Murdoch
3. The Carpathia

Page 74 .... **Visit A Viking Ship**

1. "Mother Earth"
2. Furs, skins, feathers, down, walrus teeth, rope, iron, whetstone, and slaves
3. Antiquary Nicolay Nicolyasen

Page 76 .... **Collect 'em All!**

1. There are nine links (though this is a number which could change as sites are added or deleted).
2. Click on the "Subscribe" button. That's it!
3. Click on "Search," then enter topic, and then click on "Go." Simple!

Page 77 .... **Frisbee™ Fun**

1. From back to front
2. A routine performed to music by one or more players
2. A spin not in flight

Page 78 .... **The Iditarod**℠

1. The life-saving highway for bringing in serum to Nome when diphtheria struck
2. The first woman to win the Iditarod
3. It is the award given to the last place finisher in the Iditarod.

Page 79 .... **Learn about 4-H**

1. Head, Heart, Hands, and Health
2. 2,000 to 2,800 acres
3. Nebraska

Page 80 .... **Crazy Cartoons!**

1. 24
2. Great Dane
3. The storyboard

Page 81 .... **Perfect Pictures**

1. 400 speed film captures light faster than 100 or 200 speed film.
2. The Greek words meaning "light writer."
3. No, not film as we know it. A CCD, charge-coupled device, stores the picture and software interprets it onto the screen.

Page 82 .... **Sports for Kids**

1. "Youppi"
2. Spokane, WA
3. 140-65-0

Page 83 .... **You Go, Girl!**

1. Swing dancing, traveling, and exercising
2. *Stories From My Life* and *Becoming Myself: True Stories About Learning from Life*
3. Yes, they can help lower your blood cholesterol level

Page 84 .... **Yo-yos for Everyone**

1. The Grand Ole Opry in Nashville, TN
2. Chico, CA and Tucson, AZ
3. All tricks performed on first attempt receive 5 points.
   A successful second attempt, if necessary, receives 3 points.

Page 86 .... **African Heroes**

1. Over 300
2. 2nd Lieutenant
3. To train black pilots and airmen

Page 87 .... **American Inventors**

1. Thomas Alva Edison
2. Douglas Englebart
3. Inventing velcro

Page 88 .... **Ancient Olympics**

1. 776 BC
2. Nothing, they usually competed without clothes!
3. No, they were forbidden with the punishment of death. However, Virgin maidens were allowed as spectators.

Page 89 .... **Creating A Car**

1. A jet engine plant in 1953
2. Body and White Stamping Assembly, Trim, and Chassis and Final
3. Because it stopped the driver from being "dashed" by flying stones when the main mode of transport was horse carriages

Page 90 .... **Discover Flight at the Air and Space Museum**

1. Sputnik
2. Flying faster than the speed of sound
3. 70%

Page 91 .... **Protect Your Invention**

1. Intellectual
2. The formula for Coca-Cola™
3. Register a copyright

Page 92 .... **The Natural History Museum of London**

1. Meteoroids are comet and asteroid debris still in space. When the debris hits Earth it becomes meteorites. (Found in *Cosmic Football*)
2. Egg thief
3. In the Museum's West Lawn

Page 93 .... **The Nobel Prize**

1. In 1867 he patented dynamite.
2. Physics, Chemistry, Literature, Physiology, Medicine, Peace, and the Economic Sciences
3. He founded The League of Nations.

Page 94 .... **Success: The Gallery of Achievement**

1. September 1984
2. Alabama State Teachers College
3. Eureka, Alaska

Page 95 .... Unexplained Discoveries

1. The Anaconda
2. $1000 fine and 5 years in jail
3. The Great Pyramid of Khufu in Giza, Egypt

Page 96 .... Wow! What a Museum!

1. 1969
2. Bernard R. Maybeck
3. 3601 Lyon Street

Page 98 .... A Whale of a Time!

1. 18 meters long (59.5 feet) and one metric ton
2. "To touch people's hearts and minds with the true beauty of nature"
3. To steer, turn, and stop

Page 99 .... Animals, Animals: The Electronic Zoo

1. An online magazine devoted to Greyhounds
2. American Society for the Prevention of Cruelty to Animals
3. In St. Kitts

Page 100 .... Explore National Parks

1. France
2. 277 miles long
3. The Great Smoky Mountains National Park

Page 101 .... Green Thumb's Garden

1. Annuals only live for one season or year, perennials come back year after year.
2. The Sitka Spruce (Pinus palustris) is Alaska's State Tree.
3. Horticulture

Page 102 .... Know Your Pet

1. Parrot
2. A reptile
3. No

Page 103 .... The National Severe Storms Laboratory

1. Flashes of lightning that do not strike the surface
2. In the 1870's
3. Research, operational (forecasting), and teaching

Page 104 .... Outrageous Earthquakes

1. Duck, Cover, and Hold
2. No
3. 12,000–14,000

Page 105 .... Sunny or Rainy?

1. The 13th
2. It is produced by Journal Square Interactive
3. Answer will vary depending on the day!

Page 106 .... Swimming with Sea Turtles

1. Seaweed
2. For food
3. 916 kg

Page 107 .... Trek the Zoo

1. River horse
2. Up to 120 liters
3. Large leaves

Page 110 .... All About Words

1. September 24, 1847
2. Placid—peaceful, calm. Function: adjective.
3. Bird, heard, third

Page 111 .... Animals, Myths, and Legends

1. A Native American tale
2. Angel
3. About 13½ inches tall

Page 112 .... Beverly Cleary

1. 1950
2. Ramona Forever (1984)
3. At University of California, Berkeley

Page 113 .... Games Galore

1. Attila, Mathilda, and Claude
2. "To get as much money in your piggy bank as possible"
3. 1797–1801 (See *Who is That?*)

Page 114 .... Get to Know Your World

1. Rich, gooey, black soil
2. 3 a.m.
3. Norwegian Sea and the North Sea

Page 115 .... Homework Resources

1. Metacrawler℠
2. The Supersite for Kids
3. No, he attends school.

Page 116 .... Kids' Books

1. Her son (Larry)
2. 63 years
3. E.B. White

Page 117 .... Pirates, Tropical Islands, and Treasure

1. He disappears with some of the treasure and is never seen again.
2. A porter
3. At The Admiral Benbow Inn

Page 120 .... Do You See What I See?

1. Visionary illusionist, skeptic, and magician (see *The Giants of Illusion*)
2. Matches
3. When two transparent patterns overlap, the resulting combination of both patterns is called a Moire pattern.

Page 121 .... Experience Energy

1. Coal, oil, and natural gas
2. Making electricity from water power
3. Uranium

Page 122 .... Genetic Secrets

1. Yes
2. In the DNA
3. The brain

Page 123 .... Infectious Diseases

1. The first vaccine
2. Light blue mold
3. The immune system

Page 124 .... **The Periodic Table**

1. 109
2. Dimitri Ivanovich Mendeleeve
3. Oxygen

Page 125 .... **Relics from the Past**

1. Around 245 million years ago
2. West Africa
3. In volcanic and metamorphic rocks

Page 126 .... **Satellites in Space**

1. 90 minutes
2. The sun
3. LEO travels east-west and Polar travels north-south

Page 127 .... **Science is Fun**

1. A bog is a wet spongy area that consists of decaying vegetation
2. Southeastern Tennessee
3. Between 4.2 and 4.4

Page 128 .... **Science with Beakman and Jax**

1. Pure carbon crystals
2. Bigger
3. Lightning

Page 129 .... **Space Out!**

1. MIT and Princeton
2. There are 88 constellations.
3. 120,536 km (equatorial)

Page 130 .... **Why Garbage Stinks**

1. 210 million tons of solid waste
2. Worms
3. 2–4 weeks, 200–500 years